T

GEORGIA
EXPLORER'S
BUCKET LIST

*Your Ultimate Travel Guide to Georgia's Top
Attractions*

Brinn Palmer

Disclaimer:

The information provided in *"Georgia Explorer's Bucket List: Your Ultimate Travel Guide to Georgia's Top Attractions"* is intended for general informational purposes only. While we strive to ensure the accuracy and reliability of the details within this guide, we cannot guarantee that all information is complete or up-to-date.

We strongly recommend that readers independently verify all details, including hours of operation, admission fees, transportation options, and the availability of attractions and accommodations before making any travel plans.

The inclusion of specific destinations, attractions, accommodations, or services in this guide does not imply endorsement or recommendation by the publisher. Travelers should exercise their own judgment and discretion when exploring Georgia and take necessary precautions for their safety and well-being.

The publisher disclaims any liability for any loss, injury, or inconvenience that may occur as a result of using the information presented in this guide. Travel with awareness, and enjoy discovering all that Georgia has to offer.

How to Use This Guide

This guide is your companion to exploring top attractions and hidden gems. Here's how to make the most of it:

- Browse by Destination: Explore different regions with top attractions and activities listed for each area.
- Plan Your Itinerary: Use detailed descriptions and tips to create a personalized travel plan.
- Check Practical Information: Review key details like hours of operation, fees, and transportation options before heading out.
- Personalize Your Adventure: Adapt the recommendations to fit your travel style and pace.
- Stay Updated: Double-check details like event dates or seasonal changes for the latest information.

Instruction For Using The Interactive QR Code Map

1. Open a QR code scanner app on your smartphone.
2. Allow the app to access your device's camera.
3. Position the QR code within the camera's viewfinder.
4. Scan the QR code by holding your device steady until it's detected.
5. After scanning, you will be linked to Google Maps, directing you to the exact location associated with the QR code.

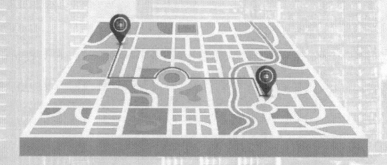

TABLE OF CONTENTS

Welcome to " Georgia Explorer's Bucket List"

Welcome to Georgia, where every corner tells a story, and each journey reveals something unforgettable. This beautiful state, known for its southern hospitality and diverse landscapes, has something for everyone—whether you're a nature lover, history buff, or city explorer.

Start your adventure in the bustling city of Atlanta, home to world-class museums, the legacy of the Civil Rights Movement, and famous landmarks like the Georgia Aquarium and Centennial Olympic Park. As you venture out, don't miss the charming city of Savannah, where cobblestone streets, centuries-old architecture, and sprawling oak trees draped in Spanish moss make you feel like you've stepped back in time.

For nature enthusiasts, Georgia's outdoor adventures are second to none. Hike the stunning trails of the Blue Ridge Mountains, kayak through the Okefenokee Swamp, or unwind on the pristine beaches of the Golden Isles. Every region has its own unique beauty, from the waterfalls and forests of North Georgia to the coastal wildlife and islands along the Atlantic.

Food lovers will be delighted by Georgia's culinary treasures, from classic Southern comfort food to farm-to-table dining experiences. Whether it's indulging in peach cobbler, sampling fresh seafood on the coast, or tasting award-winning wines in Georgia's vineyards, your taste buds are in for a treat.

This "Georgia Explorer's Bucket List" is your guide to uncovering the state's most iconic landmarks, cultural experiences, and hidden treasures. Whether you're here for a short visit or planning an extended stay, Georgia promises to leave you with lasting memories and a longing to return.

Welcome to Georgia—let the adventure begin!

A Brief History of Georgia

Georgia's rich and complex history spans centuries, from the Native American tribes who first inhabited the land to its role as a key state in the birth and development of the United States. Named after King George II of Great Britain, Georgia was founded in 1733 by British philanthropist James Oglethorpe as a refuge for debtors and a buffer against Spanish Florida.

Before European settlement, Georgia was home to indigenous groups such as the Creek and Cherokee tribes, whose influence is still felt in the state today. As one of the original 13 colonies, Georgia played a significant role in the American Revolution, although it was one of the last to join the rebellion against British rule.

In the early 19th century, Georgia expanded rapidly, driven by cotton agriculture and the forced removal of Native American populations during the infamous Trail of Tears. The state became a major player in the Confederacy during the Civil War, and the city of Atlanta's burning by General Sherman in 1864 remains a defining moment in U.S. history.

Following the war, Georgia endured the challenges of Reconstruction and the Jim Crow era. Despite these struggles, the state emerged as a key center of the Civil Rights Movement. Legendary figures like Dr. Martin Luther King Jr. and John Lewis fought for equality, leaving a lasting legacy of activism and progress in Georgia's cities, particularly Atlanta.

Today, Georgia continues to grow and evolve, balancing its deep historical roots with its modern identity as a hub for business, technology, and culture. Its history is a fascinating tale of resilience, transformation, and the ongoing pursuit of freedom and opportunity for all its people.

Why Choose Georgia for Your Vacation?

Georgia is the perfect destination for a vacation that offers a bit of everything—whether you're seeking outdoor adventures, cultural experiences, or a relaxing getaway. Here's why Georgia should top your travel list:

1. **Diverse Landscapes**
    From the rugged beauty of the Appalachian Mountains in North

Georgia to the serene coastline along the Atlantic, Georgia's natural scenery is incredibly diverse. Explore breathtaking waterfalls, hike through lush forests, or relax on golden beaches— every corner of the state offers a unique escape into nature.

2. **Rich History and Culture**
Step into the past in the historic city of Savannah, with its antebellum architecture and charming squares, or visit Atlanta to learn about Georgia's pivotal role in the Civil Rights Movement. The state's rich history is woven into its landmarks, museums, and historic homes, making it a destination where every sight tells a story.

3. **Vibrant Cities**
Atlanta, Georgia's capital, is a dynamic metropolis with world-class attractions like the Georgia Aquarium, the World of Coca-Cola, and the Martin Luther King Jr. National Historical Park. It's also a hub for art, music, and entertainment. Savannah and Augusta bring their own charm, blending modern comforts with historic beauty and southern hospitality.

4. **Outdoor Adventures**
For those who love the outdoors, Georgia is a paradise. Go hiking in the Blue Ridge Mountains, paddle through the swamps of the Okefenokee, or camp under the stars in one of the state's many parks. You can even explore unique ecosystems like Cumberland Island, home to wild horses and pristine beaches.

5. **Southern Cuisine**
Georgia is a food lover's dream! Enjoy authentic Southern cuisine, from fried chicken and shrimp and grits to peach cobbler and pecan pie. The state's growing farm-to-table movement ensures you'll enjoy fresh, local flavors no matter where you dine.

6. **Year-Round Destination**
Whether you want a beach vacation in the summer, a cozy mountain retreat in the fall, or a springtime stroll through blooming gardens, Georgia is a year-round destination. The mild climate means there's always a good time to visit, and each season brings its own unique beauty and events.

7. **Family-Friendly Fun**
Georgia offers plenty of attractions for families, including the Atlanta Zoo, Stone Mountain Park, and the interactive Children's Museum of Atlanta. Kids and adults alike will enjoy the state's mix of outdoor activities, historical sites, and family-oriented events.

8. **Music, Festivals, and Entertainment**
Georgia's vibrant music scene spans country, hip-hop, rock, and everything in between. Music lovers can explore venues and festivals across the state, including the famous annual Georgia

Music Hall of Fame Awards. Additionally, Georgia hosts countless festivals celebrating everything from peaches to film, providing year-round entertainment.

Best Time to Visit Georgia for Vacation

Georgia is a year-round destination, but the best time to visit depends on the type of experience you're seeking. With its mild climate, Georgia offers something special in every season. Here's a guide to help you choose the perfect time to plan your visit:

Spring (March to May)

Best for: Outdoor activities, festivals, and mild weather

- Spring is one of the most beautiful times to visit Georgia. The weather is pleasant, with average temperatures ranging from the mid-50s°F (12°C) to the high 70s°F (25°C), making it perfect for exploring the state's parks, gardens, and outdoor attractions.
- It's also the season of blooming flowers and greenery, especially in Savannah, Atlanta's Botanical Garden, and the North Georgia mountains.
- Many of Georgia's famous festivals take place in spring, including the Atlanta Dogwood Festival and Savannah's St. Patrick's Day Parade, one of the largest in the U.S.

Summer (June to August)

Best for: Beach vacations and water activities

- Summer in Georgia can get hot, with temperatures often reaching the 90s°F (32°C) or higher, especially in July and August. However, this is the perfect time to enjoy the state's coastal areas and lakes.
- The Golden Isles, including Jekyll Island and St. Simons Island, are ideal for beachgoers. You can also cool off with water activities like kayaking, paddleboarding, or boating.
- Summer is a great time for family vacations with visits to Georgia's theme parks, including Six Flags Over Georgia and Wild Adventures.

Fall (September to November)

Best for: Scenic drives, fall foliage, and harvest festivals

- Fall is one of the most popular times to visit Georgia, especially for those who love outdoor activities and fall festivals. The weather is cooler, with temperatures ranging from the mid-60s°F (18°C) to the low 80s°F (27°C) in September, gradually cooling as the season progresses.
- The fall foliage in North Georgia, particularly in the Blue Ridge Mountains, is stunning. This is the perfect time for hiking, scenic drives, and apple picking in places like Ellijay.
- Fall festivals abound, celebrating everything from pumpkins to peanuts, including the Georgia Apple Festival and the Georgia National Fair.

Winter (December to February)

Best for: Holiday events, cozy mountain retreats, and fewer crowds

- Winter in Georgia is generally mild, with temperatures ranging from the 30s°F (1°C) in the mountains to the 50s°F (10°C) in the southern parts of the state. While snow is rare in most areas, the North Georgia mountains can experience light snowfall, making for a cozy winter escape.
- Winter is a great time to visit the state's charming small towns and enjoy festive holiday events like the Stone Mountain Christmas or Savannah's Holiday Tour of Homes.
- If you prefer fewer crowds and lower accommodation rates, winter is an excellent time to explore cities like Atlanta and Savannah at a more relaxed pace.

Summary: Best Time to Visit

- **Spring** and **fall** are generally the best times to visit Georgia, with comfortable weather and a variety of festivals and outdoor activities to enjoy.
- If you're looking for a beach getaway or water-based adventures, **summer** is ideal, though be prepared for hotter temperatures.
- For those seeking holiday festivities, peaceful mountain retreats, or lower travel costs, **winter** offers a quieter, cozier vacation experience.

No matter when you visit, Georgia's charm, natural beauty, and rich culture ensure you'll have a memorable trip!

Practical Information

Planning a trip to Georgia is an exciting adventure, and having practical information at your fingertips can help ensure that your visit is smooth and enjoyable. From transportation options to local customs and important travel tips, this guide provides essential information for making the most of your time in the Peach State.

Getting to Georgia
Georgia is well-connected to other states and countries, making it easy to reach by air, car, or even train.
- **By Air:** The primary gateway to Georgia is Hartsfield-Jackson Atlanta International Airport (ATL), one of the busiest airports in the world. It offers numerous domestic and international flights, making it a convenient hub for travelers. Savannah/Hilton Head International Airport (SAV) is another option for those visiting Georgia's coastal regions.
- **By Car:** Georgia is accessible via several major highways, including Interstate 75, Interstate 85, and Interstate 95, which connect the state to neighboring regions. Driving into Georgia is a great option if you plan on exploring various parts of the state.
- **By Train:** Amtrak offers rail service to several Georgia cities, including Atlanta, Savannah, Gainesville, and Toccoa, providing a scenic and leisurely way to travel.
- **By Bus:** Greyhound and Megabus operate routes to and from Georgia, with major hubs in Atlanta and other large cities.

Getting Around Georgia
Georgia offers a variety of transportation options depending on your destination and how you prefer to travel.
- **Car Rentals:** Renting a car is one of the best ways to explore Georgia, especially if you plan to visit destinations outside of the

major cities, such as the North Georgia mountains or the coastal areas. Car rental services are available at major airports and in most large cities.

- **Public Transportation:** In Atlanta, the Metropolitan Atlanta Rapid Transit Authority (MARTA) provides convenient public transportation, including buses and trains, that connect many parts of the city and surrounding suburbs. Savannah also offers a limited public bus system (Chatham Area Transit, or CAT) for visitors exploring the historic district and nearby areas.
- **Taxis and Ridesharing:** Taxis are available in major cities like Atlanta, Savannah, and Augusta, though ridesharing services such as Uber and Lyft are often more convenient and readily available.
- **Bicycling and Walking:** Many cities in Georgia, particularly Savannah and Athens, are highly walkable. If you prefer to explore on two wheels, some cities have bike rental services or bike-share programs, making it easy to see the sights at a slower pace.

What to Pack
Packing for Georgia largely depends on the season and the type of activities you plan to enjoy.
- **Spring/Fall:** Bring layers, as temperatures can fluctuate throughout the day. A light jacket or sweater is ideal for cooler mornings and evenings. Comfortable walking shoes are recommended for exploring cities or hiking.
- **Summer:** Pack lightweight, breathable clothing to handle the heat and humidity, as well as sunscreen, sunglasses, and a hat for sun protection. Comfortable sandals or walking shoes are ideal for exploring outdoors.
- **Winter:** If you're visiting in winter, pack warmer layers, especially if you'll be in northern Georgia. A jacket, scarf, and gloves may be needed for chilly mornings, but you'll likely be comfortable during the day with lighter clothing.
- **Rain Gear:** Georgia can experience rain throughout the year, particularly in the spring and summer. A lightweight rain jacket or umbrella will come in handy.

Currency and Payments
- **Currency:** The official currency in Georgia is the U.S. dollar (USD). Credit and debit cards are widely accepted, especially in cities and tourist areas. Visa, Mastercard, and American Express are commonly used.
- **ATMs:** ATMs are widely available in cities and towns across Georgia, and many hotels, stores, and restaurants accept card payments. However, it's always a good idea to carry some cash, especially when visiting rural areas or smaller towns where card payments might be less common.
- **Tipping:** Tipping is customary in Georgia, as it is throughout the U.S. In restaurants, a tip of 15-20% of the total bill is standard. Tipping taxi drivers, hotel staff, and tour guides is also expected, usually around 10-15% depending on the service.

Health and Safety
- **Healthcare:** Georgia has a robust healthcare system, with hospitals, clinics, and pharmacies located throughout the state. If you require medical assistance during your stay, Atlanta and other large cities have top-rated hospitals, while smaller towns have clinics to meet most healthcare needs.
- **Travel Insurance:** It's advisable to have travel insurance that covers medical expenses in case of an emergency. U.S. citizens should ensure their health insurance plans cover them during travel, while international visitors may want to purchase additional coverage.
- **Safety:** Georgia is generally a safe state for travelers, but it's always important to follow standard safety precautions. In cities, be mindful of your surroundings and keep personal belongings secure, particularly in busy areas. When hiking or exploring outdoor areas, make sure to stay on marked trails and carry water to stay hydrated.

Local Laws and Customs
- **Smoking:** Smoking is prohibited in most public places in Georgia, including restaurants, bars, and public buildings. Be sure to check for designated smoking areas if needed.
- **Alcohol:** The legal drinking age in Georgia is 21. Alcohol is widely available at restaurants, bars, and liquor stores, though

some counties (especially in more rural areas) may have restrictions on alcohol sales, particularly on Sundays.

- **Cultural Etiquette:** Southerners are known for their hospitality, and Georgians are no exception. It's customary to greet people with a friendly "hello" or "good morning." In smaller towns, you may notice people being more open to conversation, and politeness is valued in most interactions.

Time Zone
Georgia operates on Eastern Standard Time (EST) and observes Daylight Saving Time, which begins on the second Sunday in March and ends on the first Sunday in November.

Emergency Information
- **Emergency Services:** In case of an emergency, dial 911 for police, fire, or medical assistance.
- **Non-Emergency Services:** For non-urgent medical issues, many cities have urgent care centers that offer walk-in services. Pharmacies are also widely available for over-the-counter medications.

Electricity
Georgia, like the rest of the U.S., uses 120V electricity and Type A/B outlets. International visitors may need to bring a power adapter to charge their devices.

Language
English is the primary language spoken in Georgia. In major cities and tourist areas, you'll also find some services available in Spanish, but knowing basic English phrases will be helpful for most travelers.

Madison Square

Location: 332 Bull St, Savannah, GA 31401, United States
Plus code: 3WF4+CC Savannah, Georgia, USA
Opening hours: Open 24 hours
Description: Madison Square is a prominent historic site in Savannah, Georgia, located within the city's well-known system of 22 squares. It features the striking Sergeant William Jasper Monument, dedicated to the Revolutionary War hero, which serves as the centerpiece of the square. Visitors to Madison Square will find detailed plaques and interpretive signs offering insights into Savannah's rich historical narrative, including references to General Sherman's headquarters during the Civil War and his infamous March to the Sea. The square is lined with classic Savannah flora, including hanging trees and meticulously maintained shrubbery, making it an excellent spot for a quiet stroll or photography. Madison Square's historic buildings surrounding the square add to its charm and cultural significance, offering a serene escape in the midst of Savannah's bustling city streets.

Nearby Attractions: Madison Square is close to other famous Savannah squares, including Monterey Square and Pulaski Square. The Savannah College of Art and Design (SCAD) buildings are also within walking distance, adding a modern artistic touch to the historic surroundings.

Important Information for Visitors: While the square is open 24 hours a day, it is recommended to visit during daylight to fully appreciate the details of the plaques and monuments.

Centennial Olympic Park

Location: Atlanta, GA 30313, United States
Plus code: QJ64+5Q Atlanta, Georgia, USA
Contact: +1 404-223-4000
Website: www.gwcca.org
Opening hours:
Monday to Sunday: 7 am – 11 pm

Description: Centennial Olympic Park is a central landmark in Atlanta, Georgia, created as a legacy of the 1996 Summer Olympics. The park spans 22 acres and offers a combination of open green space, historical significance, and attractions. Among its key features is the Fountain of Rings, a popular spot for families and visitors, particularly during warmer months when children can play in the water. The park also showcases artifacts from the Olympics and is well-manicured, with landscaping that contributes to its pleasant atmosphere. Although the park is a lovely area for walking, taking in the views, and enjoying the city, there are challenges related to homelessness in the area, which authorities are actively managing to ensure a safe environment for all visitors. The surrounding attractions, such as the SkyView Ferris Wheel, offer panoramic views of the city, further enhancing the park's appeal. The area includes a small playground for children and picnic spaces, making it a suitable spot for family outings. It is recommended to visit in the evening when the weather cools down, and there is a lively atmosphere around the park.

Nearby Attractions: The park is within walking distance of several notable attractions, including the Georgia Aquarium, the World of Coca-Cola, and the College Football Hall of Fame. SkyView Atlanta, a nearby Ferris wheel, offers elevated views of the city and is a popular attraction for visitors.

Important Information for Visitors: The park is open daily from 7 am to 11 pm. It is advised to bring a towel and a change of clothes if you plan to use the Fountain of Rings. Parking is available on nearby streets at a low cost, and scooter rentals are available for those who want to explore the area further.

Georgia Aquarium

Location: 225 Baker St NW, Atlanta, GA 30313, United States
Plus code: QJ73+9X Atlanta, Georgia, USA
Contact: +1 404-581-4000
Website: www.georgiaaquarium.org

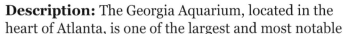

Opening hours:
Saturday: 9 am – 5 pm
Sunday: 9 am – 8 pm
Monday (Labor Day): 9 am – 8 pm (Holiday hours)
Tuesday to Thursday: 9 am – 6 pm
Friday: 9 am – 8 pm

Description: The Georgia Aquarium, located in the heart of Atlanta, is one of the largest and most notable aquariums in the world. It features a diverse range of marine life, including whale sharks, dolphins, and sea lions. Interactive exhibits and educational shows such as the Dolphin and Sea Lion performances make it an ideal destination for both families and solo travelers. The Ocean Voyager exhibit, home to the whale sharks, is a key highlight of the aquarium. Visitors are encouraged to allocate 3-4 hours to fully explore the aquarium, which offers a unique opportunity to engage with the wonders of aquatic life. The facility is well-maintained, providing a clean and safe environment for all. Tickets can be easily purchased online, and it is recommended to book in advance to avoid higher prices on the day of your visit.

Nearby Attractions: The aquarium is conveniently located near Centennial Olympic Park, the World of Coca-Cola, and the College Football Hall of Fame, making it an integral part of Atlanta's popular downtown tourist circuit.

Important Information for Visitors: It is advisable to wear comfortable shoes due to the extensive walking involved. For families with young children, strollers or carriers are recommended. Be aware of your surroundings when outside the aquarium, especially near public playgrounds. The aquarium offers food services inside, but prices are high, so planning ahead for meals is suggested.

The Big Oak

Location: 124 E Monroe St, Thomasville, GA 31792, United States

Plus code: R2R9+C7 Thomasville, Georgia, USA

Contact: +1 229-236-0053

Website: bigoak.rose.net

Opening hours:

Monday to Sunday: 8 am – 6 pm

Description: The Big Oak in Thomasville, Georgia, is a remarkable live oak tree, estimated to be nearly 340 years old. Standing as a living testament to the passage of time, it was already thriving during the signing of the U.S. Constitution. This massive tree, with its sprawling branches supported by chains and bars, is a mesmerizing sight. The tree is home to an impressive array of resurrection ferns, which add to its natural beauty. Visitors can enjoy the tranquility of the space, standing in admiration of this ancient giant. A unique feature of The Big Oak is its photo opportunity, where visitors can dial a phone number posted on a sign and receive a free picture taken from a camera mounted on a nearby telephone pole. There is no entrance fee, making it a highly accessible attraction for all. The tree's location in historic downtown Thomasville is surrounded by other beautiful trees, but The Big Oak stands out for its sheer size and age.

Nearby Attractions: The Big Oak is located in Thomasville's historic downtown, making it an easy walk from several other points of interest, including charming shops, local restaurants, and historic landmarks such as the Thomas County Museum of History.

Important Information for Visitors: The site is free to visit, and there is ample parking available nearby. If driving a large vehicle or motor home, it is recommended to check the route on Google Maps in satellite mode to avoid low-clearance branches.

Fort Frederica National Monument

Location: 6515 Frederica Rd, St Simons Island, GA 31522, United States
Plus code: 6JF5+M5 St Simons Island, Georgia, USA
Contact: +1 904-638-3639
Website: nps.gov
Opening hours:
Monday to Sunday: 9 am – 5 pm

Description: Fort Frederica National Monument is a historic site on St. Simons Island, Georgia, commemorating a significant chapter in early American colonial history. Established by James Oglethorpe in 1736, the fort and the town surrounding it were strategic during the colonial conflicts between Britain and Spain. Today, visitors can explore the remnants of the fort and the surrounding ruins of the old town. The site offers an immersive look at colonial life, with informative signs detailing the history of the area. The visitor center features a small museum with historical artifacts, educational exhibits, and a store with books and memorabilia. There are accessible pathways, clean restrooms, and helpful park staff available to answer questions and enhance your visit. Bug spray is highly recommended due to the presence of mosquitoes, especially during warmer months. Admission is free, making it an easily accessible destination for all.

Nearby Attractions: Fort Frederica is located on scenic St. Simons Island, which boasts other attractions such as Christ Church, one of Georgia's oldest religious structures, and the St. Simons Island Lighthouse, both of which are just a short drive away.

Important Information for Visitors: Guided tours are highly recommended for a more in-depth experience. No reservations are required, and the park is family-friendly with engaging exhibits and dress-up opportunities for children.

Savannah Historic District

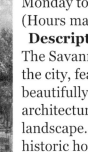

Location: 301 Martin Luther King Jr Blvd, Savannah, GA 31401, United States (Located in Savannah Visitor Center)
Plus code: 3WG2+C9 Savannah, Georgia, USA
Contact: +1 912-944-0455
Opening hours:
Monday to Sunday: 9 am – 5:30 pm
(Hours may differ on holidays)

Description:
The Savannah Historic District is the cultural heart of the city, featuring a blend of cobblestone streets, beautifully preserved 18th- and 19th-century architecture, and over 20 public squares that dot the landscape. The district is steeped in history, from historic homes like the Mercer-Williams House and Juliette Gordon Low's Birthplace to iconic landmarks such as Forsyth Park and the Cathedral of St. John the Baptist. The area is walkable, with shaded streets lined by towering oaks draped in Spanish moss, creating an atmospheric backdrop for exploration. Visitors can enjoy various dining options, boutique shops, and art galleries throughout the district, with River Street and the City Market being popular destinations for food, shopping, and nightlife. The Savannah Historic District offers guided tours, including trolley rides, which provide a detailed historical narrative while allowing visitors to hop on and off at key points of interest.

Nearby Attractions: The district is in proximity to River Street, Forsyth Park, the Owens-Thomas House & Slave Quarters, and several museums, offering a rich array of attractions within walking distance.

Visitor Information:

- The district can be explored on foot, though trolley tours are also available for a more comprehensive experience.

- Parking is available throughout the district, but walking is the preferred method to fully experience the area's charm.

- Suitable for all ages, the area offers something for everyone, from history enthusiasts to casual tourists.

Driftwood Beach

Location: Jekyll Island, GA 31527, United States
Contact: +1 800-933-2627
Website: goldenisles.com
Description:
Driftwood Beach is a striking and serene beach located on the north end of Jekyll Island. Known for its hauntingly beautiful landscape, the beach is dotted with the skeletal remains of trees, which have been preserved by erosion. The weathered driftwood makes for an extraordinary and photogenic setting, especially at sunrise, when the sun rises across the ocean, casting a warm glow on the natural sculptures. The beach is less commercialized than other spots, making it a quiet and restful destination perfect for relaxation or a scenic walk. While there are no nearby facilities such as bathrooms or pavilions, the peaceful atmosphere and unique scenery more than compensate for the lack of amenities. The beach is also ideal for photography, though swimming is not recommended due to the presence of large rocks and submerged trees in the water.

Nearby Attractions: Driftwood Beach is a short distance from the Jekyll Island Historic District, the Georgia Sea Turtle Center, and the Jekyll Island Club Resort.

Visitor Information:

- **Fee:** There is a $10 entrance fee to access Jekyll Island.

- **Parking:** Street-side parking is available near a sandy path leading to the beach.

- **Best Time to Visit:** Sunrise is highly recommended for the best views and photos.

National Civil War Naval Museum

Location: 1002 Victory Dr, Columbus, GA 31901, United States
Plus Code: C2WC+P5 Columbus, Georgia, USA
Contact: +1 706-327-9798
Website: portcolumbus.org
Description:
The National Civil War Naval Museum in Columbus, Georgia, offers a unique glimpse into naval operations during the Civil War. This locally operated museum houses an extensive collection of artifacts, including original ship sections, cannons, and uniforms, along with immersive displays that provide a deep understanding of the naval warfare of that era. Visitors can walk through reconstructed sections of naval vessels, giving them an authentic sense of life aboard these historic ships. Knowledgeable staff members are available to guide guests and answer questions, making it an enriching educational experience for history enthusiasts. The museum focuses on the naval history connected to the Chattahoochee River and the city of Columbus, providing a unique local perspective on the broader conflict.

Visitor Information:

- **Admission Fee:** Admission fees vary by age, with discounts for children, seniors, and military personnel. Check the official website for details.

- **Hours of Operation:**
   o **Saturday:** 10:00 am – 4:30 pm
   o **Sunday:** 12:30 pm – 4:30 pm
   o **Monday - Friday:** 10:00 am – 4:30 pm
- **Reservation:** Not required.

- **Wait Time:** Typically no wait.

Nearby Attractions:
- Columbus Riverwalk
- The Coca-Cola Space Science Center
- The National Infantry Museum

Golden Isles Convention & Visitors Bureau

Location: 529 Beachview Dr, St Simons Island, GA 31522, United States

Plus Code: 4JP4+64 St Simons Island, Georgia, USA

Contact: +1 912-638-9014

Website: goldenisles.com

Description: The Golden Isles Convention & Visitors Bureau on St. Simons Island serves as an elegant and informative welcome center for both first-time visitors and frequent travelers. It provides brochures, maps, and detailed information on local attractions, dining, and accommodations. The knowledgeable and friendly staff are ready to assist with personalized recommendations, and visitors can browse through a collection of locally crafted gifts, books, and apparel in the on-site gift shop. The center also features art from local artists, creating a relaxed atmosphere for planning your exploration of the Golden Isles.

Visitor Information:

- **Admission Fee:** Free

- **Hours of Operation:**
  - **Saturday:** 9:00 am – 5:00 pm
  - **Sunday:** 12:00 pm – 5:00 pm
  - **Monday - Friday:** 9:00 am – 5:00 pm

Ocmulgee Mounds National Historical Park

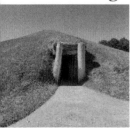

Location: 1207 Emery Hwy, Macon, GA 31217, United States

Plus Code: R9QX+75 Macon, Georgia, USA

Contact: +1 478-752-8257

Website: nps.gov

Description: Ocmulgee Mounds National Historical Park features ancient earthworks and structures constructed by Native American cultures over 12,000 years ago. The park offers a range of activities, including exploring paved and unpaved trails, visiting a museum, and viewing historic mounds and reconstructions. The visitor center includes exhibits and a film that provides historical context. The grounds are accessible via walking and biking paths, with ample opportunities to observe historical and natural features.

Visitor Information:
- **Admission Fee:** Free
- **Hours of Operation:**
  - **Saturday:** 9:00 am – 5:00 pm
  - **Sunday:** 9:00 am – 5:00 pm
  - **Monday - Friday:** 9:00 am – 5:00 pm
- **Reservation:** Not required
- **Wait Time:** Typically no wait

Nearby Attractions:
- Museum of Arts and Sciences, Macon
- Harriet Tubman Museum
- Macon Historic District

Stone Mountain Park

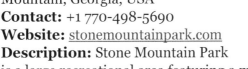

Location: 1000 Robert E Lee Blvd, Stone Mountain, GA 30083, United States
Plus Code: RV43+3W Stone Mountain, Georgia, USA
Contact: +1 770-498-5690
Website: stonemountainpark.com
Description: Stone Mountain Park is a large recreational area featuring a massive granite mountain with various activities and attractions. Visitors can hike to the summit, take a scenic skyride, enjoy a train tour around the base, or participate in seasonal festivals. The park includes picnic areas, playgrounds, and opportunities for outdoor recreation. The laser show at night is a popular event. The park is well-suited for families, with numerous amenities and activities available.

Visitor Information:
- **Admission Fee:** $41 for a day pass to all attractions; Military Pricing available
- **Hours of Operation:**
  - **Saturday:** 5:00 am – 12:00 am
  - **Sunday:** 5:00 am – 12:00 am
  - **Monday - Friday:** 5:00 am – 12:00 am
- **Reservation:** Tickets can be purchased online; recommended to avoid long lines
- **Wait Time:** Varies; expect long lines on weekends and holidays

Facilities:
- **Playground:** Available
- **Restrooms:** Clean and available around the park
- **Dog-friendliness:** Pets are allowed in some areas but not on the hiking trails or inside the park attractions
- **Picnic Area:** Numerous picnic shelters available

Nearby Attractions:
- Atlanta Botanical Garden
- Georgia Aquarium
- World of Coca-Cola

Little Cumberland Island Lighthouse

Location: Cumberland Island, Georgia, St Marys, GA 31558, United States
Plus Code: XHGP+FP St Marys, Georgia, USA

Description:

The Little Cumberland Island Lighthouse, built in 1838, is located on Little Cumberland Island, which lies just north of Cumberland Island. This historic lighthouse, with its original fourteen lamps generating a fixed light, was designed to be distinct from the revolving light of the older tower to the south. The lighthouse was in operation until 1915 and was protected by a brick wall constructed in 1874 to prevent erosion. Although the lighthouse was deactivated and the keeper's house demolished in 1968, the tower remains and was renovated between 1994 and 1998. The lighthouse is listed on the National Register of Historic Places (No. 89001407) since August 8, 1989. Little Cumberland Island is privately owned and not open to the public, limiting access to the lighthouse.

Visitor Information:

- **Access:** The lighthouse is not open to the public due to the island's private ownership. Viewing is limited from a distance.

- **Nearby Attractions:**
    - Cumberland Island National Seashore
    - St. Marys Historic District

Note: As the island is privately owned, visitors should respect the restricted access and view the lighthouse from designated areas or tours.

Georgia's Old Governor's Mansion

Location: 120 S Clarke St, Milledgeville, GA 31061, United States
Plus Code: 3QH9+VC
Milledgeville, Georgia, USA
Contact: +1 478-445-4545
Website: www.gcsu.edu

Opening Hours:
- Saturday: 10am – 4pm
- Sunday: 2pm – 4pm
- Monday (Labor Day): Closed
- Tuesday to Friday: 10am – 4pm

Description: Georgia's Old Governor's Mansion, located on the campus of Georgia College, is a historic site that offers an in-depth look into 19th-century Georgian architecture and governance. Constructed in 1838, the mansion served as the official residence of Georgia's governors until 1868. Visitors can explore well-preserved rooms and original furnishings, providing insights into the state's political and social history. Tours are conducted by knowledgeable guides who offer detailed explanations of the mansion's significance and historical context. The site also hosts special events, particularly during the holiday season when the mansion is decorated. The entry fee is between $6 and $10 for adults, with discounts available for seniors, military personnel, children, and students. Georgia College students and staff enjoy free admission.

Nearby Attractions: The mansion is situated in Milledgeville, which is also home to other historic sites and cultural attractions, including the Old Capitol Building and the Georgia College and State University campus.

Important Information for Visitors: It is highly recommended to check the museum's schedule for special events or changes in hours, especially around holidays. The mansion's tours are typically not crowded, offering a more personalized experience.

Skidaway Island State Park

Location: 52 Diamond Causeway, Savannah, GA 31411, United States
Plus Code: XW3W+WX Savannah, Georgia, USA
Contact: +1 912-598-2300
Website: gastateparks.org/SkidawayIsland

Opening Hours:

• Monday to Sunday: 7am – 10pm

Description: Skidaway Island State Park offers a serene natural escape near Savannah, Georgia. The park features extensive hiking trails, including the Slough Trail and Big Ferry Trail, which wind through salt marshes, tidal creeks, and maritime forests. These trails are well-suited for nature walks and wildlife observation, providing opportunities to see various bird species and other local wildlife. The park also includes a well-maintained campground with spacious sites, though it no longer has a pool. Visitors can enjoy picnicking in designated areas and exploring the park's interpretive center, which provides insights into the region's ecology and history. Parking is available, but a parking pass must be purchased. The park is a short drive from Savannah, making it convenient for exploring the city's historic district and River Street.

Nearby Attractions: The park's proximity to Savannah allows visitors to explore the city's historic sites and waterfront attractions.

Important Information for Visitors: Due to its location, visitors should be prepared for the possibility of mosquitoes, especially in warmer months. It is recommended to bring insect repellent.

Providence Canyon State Park

Location: 8930 Canyon Rd, Lumpkin, GA 31815, United States
Plus Code: 339P+H7 Lumpkin, Georgia, USA
Contact: +1 229-838-6202
Website: gastateparks.org/ProvidenceCanyon

Opening Hours:

• Monday to Sunday: 7am – 6pm

Description: Providence Canyon State Park, often referred to as Georgia's "Little Grand Canyon," is renowned for its striking canyon formations and colorful clay walls. The park offers a variety of trails that cater to different levels of hiking experience. The shorter trails, approximately 2 to 3 miles, provide quick yet rewarding views of the canyons, while the longer trails, which can take up to 6 hours and require a permit, offer a more extensive exploration of the area. Visitors are advised to wear sturdy, waterproof hiking boots due to the muddy conditions at the canyon floor. The park is pet-friendly and includes a playground for children, making it suitable for family outings. A gift shop and store offer souvenirs and basic amenities, though visitors should be prepared for possible issues with restrooms and bring their own water and snacks. The park also features tent camping areas. It is highly recommended to avoid climbing on the canyon walls to help preserve these ancient formations. The park provides a unique outdoor experience with panoramic views and a range of hiking opportunities.

Nearby Attractions: The park is a short drive from Lumpkin, where visitors can explore local amenities and attractions.

Important Information for Visitors: Ensure to carry sufficient water and snacks, particularly if hiking the longer trails. Be mindful of wildlife, including bears, and adhere to park rules to protect the natural environment.

Old Fort Jackson

Location: 1 Fort Jackson Rd, Savannah, GA 31404, United States
Plus Code: 3XJ7+QM Savannah, Georgia, USA
Contact: +1 912-232-3945
Website: chsgeorgia.org

Opening Hours:

• Monday to Sunday: 9am – 4pm

   Description: Old Fort Jackson is a well-preserved 19th-century fortification located on the Savannah River. Originally constructed to protect Savannah from potential waterborne attacks, the fort features a range of historic exhibits, including cannons and military artifacts. Visitors can enjoy guided tours led by knowledgeable staff dressed in period costumes, who provide engaging historical narratives and demonstrations. The fort also offers

live demonstrations, such as cannon firings, which are scheduled throughout the day. A small gift shop on-site provides snacks, beverages, and souvenirs. For comfort, especially after rain, it is recommended to use bug spray and wear long, loose clothing to avoid mosquitoes. The fort's strategic location provides excellent views of the river and its surroundings.

Nearby Attractions: Old Fort Jackson is situated near other historic sites in Savannah, offering additional opportunities for exploration and sightseeing.

Important Information for Visitors: Due to the fort's location over a swampy area, it is advisable to use insect repellent and dress appropriately for the weather. There is no need for reservations, and the fort is accessible during its regular hours of operation.

Phinizy Swamp Nature Park

Location: 1858 Lock and Dam Rd, Augusta, GA 30906, United States
Plus Code: 92MJ+RX Augusta, Georgia, USA
Contact: +1 706-828-2109
Website: phinizycenter.org

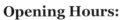

Opening Hours:

- Monday to Sunday: 7am – 7pm

Description: Phinizy Swamp Nature Park is a serene natural area offering a variety of walking trails through diverse wetlands and wooded environments. Visitors can explore elevated boardwalks and traditional trails, providing opportunities to observe local wildlife including alligators, birds, and insects. The park features a small playground and picnic areas for relaxation. Restrooms are available at both the park entrance and the main campus. The park is free to enter, making it an accessible option for nature enthusiasts. Trails are generally flat, suitable for casual walks, and the park is pet-friendly. For safety, be cautious of potential hazards like rotten boardwalk boards, and dress in layers as temperatures can vary throughout the day.

Nearby Attractions: The park's proximity to Augusta makes it a convenient stop for travelers heading to or from the regional airport.

Important Information for Visitors: The park is free to enter, and no reservations are required. Ensure to bring water and wear suitable clothing for outdoor activities. The visitor center may occasionally be closed, but the park remains accessible.

F.D. Roosevelt State Park

Location: 2970 GA-190, Pine Mountain, GA 31822, United States
Plus Code: R5VC+QG Pine Mountain, Georgia, USA
Contact: +1 706-663-4858
Website: gastateparks.org

Opening Hours:

• Monday to Sunday: 8am – 10pm

Description: F.D. Roosevelt State Park offers a range of outdoor activities set within a picturesque landscape. The park features well-maintained trails, including options for hiking and geocaching, and is known for its scenic beauty around Lake Delanor. Visitors can enjoy the Lake Franklin Event Center, which provides ample parking and excellent views, making it suitable for various events. The park also offers cottage accommodations with full amenities, providing a comfortable stay amidst nature. Facilities include clean bathrooms, showers, and spacious campsites, with an emphasis on maintaining a serene environment. The park is pet-friendly and ideal for nature lovers seeking relaxation or outdoor adventures.

Nearby Attractions: Lake Delanor within the park offers opportunities for tranquil mornings and sunset views, while the surrounding trails provide additional exploration options.

Important Information for Visitors: The park is free to enter, and no reservations are required for general park access. However, booking is recommended for cottage stays and event center use. Ensure to bring appropriate gear for outdoor activities and check weather conditions before planning your visit.

Fun Spot America Theme Parks — Atlanta

Location: 1675 GA-85, Fayetteville, GA 30214, United States
Plus Code: FHWC+GR Fayetteville, Georgia, USA
Contact: +1 407-363-3867
Website: funspotamericaatlanta.com

Opening Hours:

- Saturday: 10am – 10pm
- Sunday: 10am – 10pm
- Monday (Labor Day): 10am – 8pm
- Tuesday: 11am – 6pm
- Wednesday: 11am – 6pm
- Thursday: 11am – 6pm
- Friday: 11am – 6pm

Description: Fun Spot America Theme Parks in Atlanta offers a variety of attractions suitable for all ages. Notable for its standout ride, Arie Force One, which is frequently praised by coaster enthusiasts, the park features a mix of thrill rides, simple attractions, and arcade games. The park is known for its well-maintained rides and friendly staff. It provides free parking and generally has shorter wait times, especially on weekdays. The park also has standard food options and water refill stations. Its compact size and manageable crowds make it a convenient choice for a fun day out, especially for families with young children.

Nearby Attractions: The park's location offers easy access to other Fayetteville amenities, though it primarily serves as a standalone entertainment destination.

Important Information for Visitors: Reservations are not typically required, but visiting during weekdays or off-peak times can enhance the experience. Be sure to check the park's website for any updates on operating hours or special events.

Fort McAllister State Park

Location: 3894 Fort McAllister Rd, Richmond Hill, GA 31324, United States
Plus Code: VRR3+FM Richmond Hill, Georgia, USA
Contact: +1 912-727-2339
Website: gastateparks.org

Opening Hours:

- Saturday: 7am – 10pm
- Sunday: 7am – 10pm
- Monday (Labor Day): 7am – 10pm
- Tuesday: 7am – 10pm
- Wednesday: 7am – 10pm
- Thursday: 7am – 10pm
- Friday: 7am – 10pm

Description: Fort McAllister State Park, located near Savannah, Georgia, offers a blend of historical significance and natural beauty. The park features a well-preserved Civil War fort and reconstructed historical buildings, providing a glimpse into the past. It is accessible and manageable for visitors of all mobility levels. The park is also known for its spacious and level campsites, which include amenities such as 50 amp service and sewer connections. While there is no playground directly in the campground, there are well-maintained playgrounds in the day-use and cottage areas. Visitors often spot wildlife, including deer, and appreciate the park's clean facilities and helpful staff. The park's scenic vistas and well-kept grounds make it a relaxing destination for history enthusiasts and nature lovers alike.

Nearby Attractions: The park's proximity to Savannah allows for easy access to additional historic and recreational sites.

Important Information for Visitors: The park is known for its friendly and accommodating staff. In case of severe weather, such as hurricanes, the park may issue mandatory evacuations and provide refunds. Visitors are encouraged to check the park's website or contact staff for any updates on conditions or potential closures.

Reynolds Square

Location: 32 Abercorn St, Savannah, GA 31401, United States
Plus Code: 3WH6+P6 Savannah, Georgia, USA
Contact: +1 912-651-6610

Opening Hours: : Open 24 hours daily
Description: Reynolds Square is a historic public square in Savannah, Georgia, designed by James Oglethorpe in 1733. Originally named Lower New Square, it was renamed in the 1750s in honor of John Reynolds, the first Royal Governor of Georgia. The square features a statue of John Wesley, the founder of Methodism, at its center. It is a peaceful and beautifully maintained area in the heart of the city, popular with both locals and visitors. The square is surrounded by notable landmarks including The Old Pink House and The Lucas Theater. It offers a serene environment with the added charm of Savannah's historic architecture.

Nearby Attractions:
- The Old Pink House
- The Lucas Theater

Important Information for Visitors: Reynolds Square is open 24 hours, but visitors should be aware of varying conditions. While it is a historically and visually appealing area, experiences can differ, and issues related to homelessness have been noted. Visitors are encouraged to remain vigilant and exercise caution, particularly when visiting during off-hours. The square is often lively, especially during events like the Saint Patrick's Day Parade, which adds to its vibrant atmosphere.

Historic Steps

Location: 207b E River St, Savannah, GA 31401, United States
Plus Code: 3WJ6+9M Savannah, Georgia, USA

Opening Hours: Open 24 hours daily

Description: The Historic Steps are a notable feature on River Street in Savannah. These steep, uneven steps were designed in the 1730s by James Oglethorpe. Legend has it that their irregular height was intended to slow down potential invaders such as pirates. The steps are constructed from various materials, including rocks used as ballast in ships, adding historical and architectural interest. The steps are accessible for climbing, though they are steep and uneven, which can make them challenging and potentially hazardous. Visitors should use handrails and exercise caution, especially if they are unsteady or have mobility issues.

Nearby Attractions:
- River Street
- Various historic buildings along the waterfront

Important Information for Visitors: The Historic Steps are free to visit and open around the clock. Due to their uneven construction, they may be difficult for those with mobility issues and should be navigated with care. The steps are best enjoyed during daylight hours for safety reasons.

Jimmy Carter National Historical Park

Location: 300 N Bond St, Plains, GA 31780, United States
Plus Code: 2JP4+GX Plains, Georgia, USA

Opening Hours: 10 am–5 pm Daily
Description: The Jimmy Carter National Historical Park offers a comprehensive look at the life and career of the 39th President of the United States, Jimmy Carter. The park includes several key sites, such as the Plains High School, where both Jimmy and Rosalynn Carter attended and met. It also features the Carters' boyhood home, the Billy Carter service station, and various other locations important to Carter's life and presidency. Exhibits cover his time as governor, president, and his work after leaving office. Visitors can explore memorabilia, historical sites,

and learn about Carter's significant contributions to society. The park is well-preserved, and admission is free.

Nearby Attractions:
- The Buffalo Cafe
- Plain Peanuts and General Store

Important Information for Visitors: The park is free to visit and offers a variety of historical sites within walking distance in the town of Plains. It is recommended to visit on a pleasant day to fully enjoy the outdoor sites. The park provides an insightful look into the life and legacy of Jimmy Carter, with exhibits and historical information spanning his entire career.

Fountain of Rings

Location: 265 Park Ave W NW, Atlanta, GA 30313, United States
Plus Code: QJ54+QV Atlanta, Georgia, USA
Located in: Centennial Olympic Park

Opening Hours: 7 am–11 pm Daily
Description: The Fountain of Rings is a prominent water feature located in Centennial Olympic Park, celebrated for its dynamic water shows that sync with music. This interactive fountain provides a scenic and engaging experience, particularly for families with children who can enjoy playing in the splash pad. The fountain also offers beautiful views and is situated near other attractions such as the Ferris wheel and the Georgia Aquarium. The park is clean and well-maintained, with ample seating and picnic spots available.

Nearby Attractions:
- Centennial Olympic Park
- Georgia Aquarium
- Ferris Wheel

Important Information for Visitors: The fountain features daily shows and performances set to music, creating an entertaining experience for visitors. While the area is generally well-kept, it is advisable to be aware of potential encounters with homeless individuals in the vicinity. Parking is available but may require a fee. The fountain is a notable part of the park's 1996 Olympic legacy and offers a pleasant spot to relax and enjoy the surroundings.

Barbie Beach

Location: 4397-4679 GA-16, Senoia, GA 30276, United States
Plus Code: 89H5+C8 Senoia, Georgia, USA

Opening Hours: Open 24hrs

Description: Barbie Beach is a quirky roadside attraction known for its whimsical displays featuring Barbie and Ken dolls in playful and imaginative scenarios. Located along GA-16, this small, home-based display includes various scenes with dolls engaged in humorous or imaginative activities. It is not a formal tourist attraction but rather a charming and nostalgic art piece created by a local family for passing motorists to enjoy. Due to its location on a narrow road and ongoing construction, parking might be a bit of a walk away. It's best enjoyed as a brief stop while driving by rather than a destination.

Nearby Attractions:

• Senoia, GA (a charming small town with local shops and eateries)

Important Information for Visitors: This display is meant to be a light-hearted and nostalgic experience rather than a major attraction. Due to construction in the area, parking may be a bit inconvenient, and visitors might need to walk a short distance to view the display. It's recommended for those passing through who appreciate quirky roadside art.

Goliath

Location: 275 Riverside Pkwy, Austell, GA 30168, United States
Plus Code: QF92+M2 Austell, Georgia, USA
Located in: Six Flags Over Georgia

Opening Hours: 11 am – 8 pm

Description: Goliath is a towering B&M Hyper Coaster renowned for its intense airtime and impressive length. As one of the standout rides at Six Flags Over Georgia, it features a series of exhilarating drops and airtime hills that offer a thrilling experience. The ride uniquely extends beyond the park boundaries, providing riders with dramatic views. Although it may have occasional rattles, they are generally minimal and do not detract significantly from the experience. The ride is celebrated for its smoothness and overall excitement, making it a must-experience attraction for thrill-seekers. It's particularly enjoyable both from the front and back rows.

Nearby Attractions:

- Six Flags Over Georgia (a major amusement park with various other rides and entertainment options)

Important Information for Visitors: Goliath is highly recommended for its thrilling ride experience. It is best to visit during less busy times for shorter wait times. Always check the ride's operational status as it may be closed for maintenance or other reasons.

Kadie the Cow

Location: 1000 Bay Ave, Columbus, GA 31901, United States
Plus Code: F283+CJ Columbus, Georgia, USA
Located in: Woodruff Riverfront Park

Opening Hours: Open 24 hours

Description: Kadie the Cow is a beloved landmark situated along the banks of the Chattahoochee River in Woodruff Riverfront Park. As a cherished icon of Columbus, Kadie originally gained fame as a mascot for the Kinnett plant milk and has been a local favorite for many years. The statue stands proudly as part of the Dragonfly Trail, offering a nostalgic touch to visitors. It is conveniently located near park facilities, including restrooms, making it a pleasant spot to visit during a walk or picnic. Kadie's presence continues to evoke fond memories for both locals and visitors alike.

Nearby Attractions:

- Woodruff Riverfront Park (features scenic views and walking paths along the Chattahoochee River)

Important Information for Visitors: Kadie the Cow is easily accessible and can be visited at any time. Parking may be challenging during peak times, such as weekends or special events. It is recommended to visit during off-peak hours for a more relaxed experience.

Southern Forest World

Location: 1440 N Augusta Ave, Waycross, GA 31503, United States
Plus Code: 6JM8+XP
Waycross, Georgia, USA

Opening Hours: 10 am–3 pm
- **Sunday:** Closed
- **Description:** Southern Forest World is an educational and family-friendly attraction focused on forestry and the uses of trees in everyday life. The museum features a variety of displays, including interactive exhibits on wildlife, taxidermy, and forestry. Highlights include the large playground, outdoor activities, and a gift shop. The museum also offers insights into the history and industry of forestry in the South. Visitors can enjoy a clean and accessible environment with wheelchair access available at the entrance and to outdoor areas.

Nearby Attractions:

- Various outdoor activities and playgrounds within the museum grounds

Important Information for Visitors:

- **Admission:** Entry for adults ranges from $1 to $5. Children aged 5 and under are free. A one-year family pass is available for $30.

- **Facilities:** Includes public restrooms, a gift shop, and interactive exhibits.

For the most accurate information, check the museum's website or contact them directly before planning your visit.

Delta Flight Museum

Location: 1060 Delta Blvd, Atlanta, GA 30354, United States
Plus Code: MH3J+X2 Atlanta, Georgia, USA
Website: deltamuseum.org
Contact: +1 404-715-7886

Opening Hours: 10 am–4 pm
- **Sunday:** Closed

Description: The Delta Flight Museum offers an engaging exploration of aviation history with a focus on Delta Airlines. The museum is divided into two main exhibits: The Prop Era and The Jet Era, showcasing the evolution of aircraft and air travel. Highlights include the opportunity to explore a real Boeing 747, interactive exhibits for children, and a wealth of information on the history of Delta Airlines. The museum provides a comprehensive look at the advancement of aviation technology and the role of Delta in that progress.

Nearby Attractions:

- Delta General Offices

- Hartsfield-Jackson Atlanta International Airport

Important Information for Visitors:

- **Admission Price:** Approximately $55 for a family of five.

- **Facilities:** Includes interactive exhibits, historical displays, and flight simulators.

- **Accessibility:** Difficult to access on foot due to lack of sidewalks. Parking is available.

- **LGBTQ+ Friendly**

Reservation Information: Reservations are recommended, especially for larger groups or during peak times.

For the most current information, including any changes to hours or admission prices, please visit the museum's website or contact them directly.

Oglethorpe Square

Location: 127 Abercorn St, Savannah, GA 31401, United States
Plus Code: 3WH5+2X Savannah, Georgia, USA
Website: savannahga.gov
Contact: +1 912-234-2273

Opening Hours: Open 24 hours

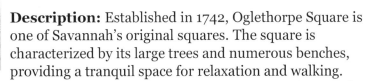

Description: Established in 1742, Oglethorpe Square is one of Savannah's original squares. The square is characterized by its large trees and numerous benches, providing a tranquil space for relaxation and walking. While it lacks statues or monuments, the surrounding area features both residential and commercial buildings. Notable nearby is the Owens-Thomas House, an English Regency-style house museum built in 1819, located on one of the Trustee lots.

Nearby Attractions:

- Owens-Thomas House & Slave Quarters

- Historic Savannah Ghost Tours

Important Information for Visitors:

- Parking can be challenging, so walking is recommended.

- The square is a frequent stop on ghost tours, offering historical insights and local lore.

- General Oglethorpe's statue is located in a different square nearby.

For the most current information, including any potential changes to nearby attractions or services, please check local resources or contact the provided number.

Cannonball House

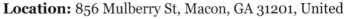

Location: 856 Mulberry St, Macon, GA 31201, United States
Plus Code: R9Q9+X5 Macon, Georgia, USA
Website: cannonballhouse.org
Contact: +1 478-745-5982

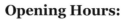

Opening Hours:

- **Saturday:** 10am – 3:30pm
- **Sunday:** Closed
- **Monday (Labor Day):** Closed
- **Tuesday to Friday:** 10am – 3:30pm

Description: The Cannonball House is a well-preserved house museum renowned for its historical significance and beautiful architecture. Named for a cannonball that remains embedded in the front of the house, it offers an intriguing glimpse into the Civil War era and the history of Macon. The museum features original furniture and artifacts, including a cannon displayed in the yard.

Nearby Attractions:
- Macon Museum of Arts and Sciences
- Hay House

Important Information for Visitors:
- Admission prices range from $6 to $10 for adults.
- The house includes a kitchen and servants' quarters as part of the tour.
- Reservations are not required but are recommended during peak times.
- The museum offers educational workshops and guided tours, which provide detailed historical insights.

Ice House Museum

Location: St Marys, GA 31558, United States
Plus Code: QG3G+QM St Marys, Georgia, USA
Website: www.nps.gov

Opening Hours:
Monday to Friday: 9am – 5pm
Closed on Saturdays and Sundays

The Ice House Museum, located on Cumberland Island, offers visitors a glimpse into the island's rich history. Situated right off the ferry dock, the museum features a range of artifacts from the early Timucuan people and provides insights into the island's historical development. Essential visitor amenities, including restrooms and a water fountain, are available on-site.

The museum's exhibits cover various aspects of Cumberland Island's past, making it a valuable stop for anyone interested in the island's heritage. Visitors should be prepared for a fair amount of walking and are advised to carry any necessary supplies for their visit. It is highly recommended to take a ferry from St. Marys to reach the island.

Nearby Attractions:

- Cumberland Island National Seashore

- Dungeness Ruins

Important Information for Visitors:

- All items brought to the island must be taken back.

- Reservations are recommended for the ferry and museum visit.

Tank Town USA

Location: 10408 Appalachian Hwy, Morganton, GA 30560, United States
Plus Code: VQQH+9C Morganton, Georgia, USA
Contact: +1 706-633-6072
Website: www.tanktownusa.com

Opening Hours:
Monday to Friday: 10am – 6pm
Saturday: 10am – 6pm
Sunday: Closed

Tank Town USA offers a unique adventure for thrill-seekers and enthusiasts. Located in Morganton, GA, this attraction provides visitors with the opportunity to drive military-style tanks, including an Armored Personnel Carrier (APC), and operate an excavator. The experience includes various packages, such as the car crush experience, where participants can drive a tank over a car and even graffiti it beforehand. Safety is a priority, and the staff, including owner Todd, ensures that all participants have a memorable and safe adventure.

The location is accessible and offers a unique outing, especially for those interested in military vehicles or looking for an unusual and exhilarating activity. Visitors are encouraged to make reservations in advance to secure their spot and to plan for the unique experience.

Nearby Attractions:

- Blue Ridge, GA: Known for its dog-friendly environment and various shops and eateries.

Important Information for Visitors:
- Reservations are recommended to ensure availability.
- Visitors should prepare for a thrilling, hands-on experience with military vehicles.
- Photography and video capturing of the experience are encouraged and facilitated by the staff.

Jarrell Plantation State Historic Site

Location: 711 Jarrell Plantation Rd, Juliette, GA 31046, United States
Plus Code: 373G+3M Juliette, Georgia, USA
Contact: +1 478-986-5172
Website: www.gastateparks.org/JarrellPlantation

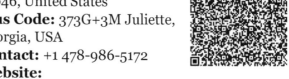

Opening Hours:
Monday: Closed
Tuesday: Closed
Wednesday: Closed
Thursday to Friday: 9am – 5pm
Saturday to Sunday: 9am – 5pm

Jarrell Plantation State Historic Site offers a glimpse into Georgia's agricultural past through the preserved 19th-century plantation. Located in Juliette, GA, the site features original and replicated historic buildings, including a cotton gin, a smokehouse, and a sawmill. Visitors can explore the expansive grounds on a self-guided tour, starting at the visitor center where an informative film provides context about the Jarrell family and the plantation's history.

The site includes farm animals such as goats and chickens, adding to the authentic experience of rural life. The walking trail around the property offers historical markers and plaques detailing the significance of various buildings. Note that the terrain includes some steep and uneven sections, so comfortable footwear is recommended.

Nearby Attractions:
- The town of Juliette, known for its historical significance and charming atmosphere.

Important Information for Visitors:
- The site hosts special events like Farm Heritage Day, which may offer additional activities and interactions.
- Reservations are not required, but it is advised to check the official website for any event schedules or changes in opening hours.
- The property is large and involves significant walking, so be prepared with appropriate footwear and supplies.

Savannah Children's Museum

Location: 655 Louisville Rd, Savannah, GA 31401, United States
Plus Code: 3VGX+CJ Savannah, Georgia, USA
Contact: +1 912-651-6823 ext. 203
Website: www.chsgeorgia.org

Opening Hours: 9am – 2pm
Sunday: Closed

The Savannah Children's Museum is located within the Georgia State Railroad Museum complex in Savannah. This outdoor museum provides a unique play experience with a variety of interactive exhibits and activities designed to engage children and stimulate their creativity. The museum features imaginative play areas, crafts, and educational stations set up in an open-air environment housed in a historic building.

Visitors will find that the museum emphasizes hands-on learning and exploration, allowing children to engage with their surroundings in a meaningful way. The museum's location within the larger railroad museum area may require some navigation, so be prepared for possible confusion regarding ticket purchase and entry points. Tickets cost $11–15 for adults, with children's admission typically being free for younger ages.

Nearby Attractions:
- Georgia State Railroad Museum, which provides additional educational exhibits and historical insights related to railroads.

Important Information for Visitors:
- The museum is entirely outdoors, so check the weather and dress appropriately.
- There is an option to check out a pass from local libraries for free admission.
- Reservations are not necessary, but be aware that tickets are sold at the entrance.

Cockspur Island Lighthouse

Location: Cockspur Island Lighthouse, Savannah, GA 31410, United States
Plus Code: 24FC+32 Savannah, Georgia, USA
Contact: +1 912-659-7777
Website: www.cockspurislandlighthouse.com

Opening Hours: 9am – 5pm
Sunday: 9am – 5pm

Cockspur Island Lighthouse is a historic lighthouse located on Cockspur Island near Savannah, Georgia. This charming lighthouse, accessible primarily by boat or by walking a long path within Fort Pulaski, offers picturesque views of the surrounding waterways and is notable for its scenic beauty, especially during sunset. Although the island itself is generally closed to the public, visitors can view the lighthouse from boat tours and nearby vantage points. The lighthouse is recognized for its small stature compared to other Georgia lighthouses and its distinctive appearance.

Nearby Attractions:

- **Fort Pulaski National Monument:** A historic fort offering guided tours and educational exhibits, located within walking distance of the lighthouse.

Important Information for Visitors:

- The lighthouse can be viewed from boat tours or from Fort Pulaski, but direct access to the island is restricted.

- Sunset offers the best opportunities for photographs.

Historic Uncle Remus Museum

Location: 214 Oak St, Eatonton, GA 31024, United States
Plus Code: 8JC6+HH Eatonton, Georgia, USA
Contact: +1 706-485-6856
Website: www.uncleremusmuseum.org

Opening Hours:
Monday to Saturday: 10am – 5pm
Sunday: 1pm – 4pm

The Historic Uncle Remus Museum offers an insightful look into the life and legacy of Joel Chandler Harris, the author behind the beloved Brer Rabbit stories. Situated in Eatonton, Georgia, the museum features three rooms dedicated to Harris's artifacts, manuscripts, and personal history. Visitors can explore exhibits that illustrate the cultural and historical context of Harris's work and his influence on American folklore. The museum is well-maintained and provides a rich educational experience about the author and his stories.

Nearby Attractions:

- **Eatonton Historic District:** Explore the charm of downtown Eatonton, which includes other historical sites and local shops.

Important Information for Visitors:

- Admission is $5 for adults and $4 for seniors.

- Photographs are not allowed inside the museum.

- Reservations are not required, but it is advisable to check for any potential schedule changes or special events.

Netherworld Haunted House

Location: 1313 Netherworld Way, Stone Mountain, GA 30087, United States
Plus Code: RV9J+CF Stone Mountain, Georgia, USA
Contact: +1 404-999-3327
Website: www.fearworld.com

Opening Hours:

Monday to Thursday: 7pm – 11pm
Friday and Saturday: 7pm – 12am
Sunday: 7pm – 11pm
(Opening hours may vary during the season; please check the website for the most current information.)

Netherworld Haunted House is renowned for its elaborate and immersive haunted attractions. Located in Stone Mountain, Georgia, this popular destination features two distinct haunted houses, offering an intense and engaging experience with highly detailed props and professional scare actors. The attraction is known for its impressive set design and well-executed scares, making it a top choice for thrill-seekers.

Guests are encouraged to purchase tickets online in advance and plan for extra travel time due to high traffic, especially during peak season. Parking is free, though it can be a considerable distance from the venue, so allow time for the walk to the entrance. The haunted houses are designed to offer a blend of traditional scares with interactive and sensory-rich environments.

Nearby Attractions:

- **Stone Mountain Park:** A large park offering hiking, attractions, and historical exhibits, providing additional activities for visitors in the area.

Important Information for Visitors:

- Tickets typically range from $21 to $30 for adults.

- Reservations are recommended, especially on weekends, to avoid long wait times.

- The experience can be very crowded, so consider purchasing a speed pass to reduce wait times.

- The venue includes a concession area and gift shop, along with photo opportunities and a bubble area for children.

Summer Waves Water Park

Location: 210 S Riverview Dr, Jekyll Island, GA 31527, United States
Plus Code: 2HQH+3M Jekyll Island, Georgia, USA
Contact: +1 912-635-2074
Website:

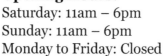

www.summerwaves.com

Opening Hours:
Saturday: 11am – 6pm
Sunday: 11am – 6pm
Monday to Friday: Closed

Description: Summer Waves Water Park offers a fun and family-friendly environment with attractions suitable for all ages. Highlights include a wave pool, lazy river, splash areas for young children, and a variety of water slides. The park features shaded seating, recliners, and snack stands, ensuring a comfortable and enjoyable experience for visitors. The park is well-maintained, and the food options are noted for being better than average.

Nearby Attractions:

- **Jekyll Island Historic District:** A historic area with charming architecture and sites, perfect for exploring before or after your visit to the water park.

Important Information for Visitors:

- An additional fee of $10 is required to access Jekyll Island, which is not included in the water park admission.

- Parking is ample but can fill up on weekends, so plan accordingly.

- The park does not currently offer discounted 2-hour passes; standard pricing applies for all-day access.

- Picnic tables are available outside the park, and you can bring your own food if you obtain a re-entry wristband.

Admission Price:

- **Adult Entry:** Generally ranges from $20 to $30, depending on the season and any special promotions.

Bald Eagle Nest

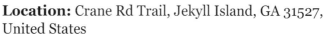

Location: Crane Rd Trail, Jekyll Island, GA 31527, United States
Plus Code: 3H3M+P6 Jekyll Island, Georgia, USA
Opening Hours: Open 24 hours daily
Description: The Bald Eagle Nest is located along the Crane Road Trail on Jekyll Island. The trail offers a scenic walk through diverse flora and fauna. Visitors have the opportunity to view the bald eagle nest, and with some luck, see one of the adult eagles perched in a nearby pine tree. The nest is marked with red tape on a tree about 20 feet up the trail, and the view of the nest can be spotted off in the distance, particularly from the south side of the trail. The trail also leads to a pond where alligators may be seen.

Nearby Attractions: The trail is a short walk from the Historic District of Jekyll Island, which provides access to additional local sites and activities.

Important Information for Visitors: The trail is accessible year-round, and no specific entry fee is required. It is recommended to visit during daylight hours for better visibility and to use a pair of binoculars for a closer view of the nest.

Helen, GA Sign

Location: 63 Chattahoochee Strasse, Helen, GA 30545, United States
Plus Code: P729+RW Helen, Georgia, USA
Opening Hours: Open 24 hours daily
Description: The Helen, GA sign is an iconic landmark located in the heart of Helen, Georgia. Positioned on Chattahoochee Strasse, this sign offers a great photo opportunity for visitors. Known for its Bavarian-style architecture and scenic

mountain backdrop, Helen provides a picturesque setting for capturing memorable photographs. The sign is part of the town's charm, which includes unique shops, local restaurants, and nearby trails. The area often attracts tourists with its vibrant atmosphere and various activities, including tubing in the river.

Nearby Attractions: Helen's downtown area features Bavarian-style buildings, vibrant flowers, and local shops. The town also offers access to scenic trails and river tubing.

Important Information for Visitors: The sign is accessible year-round without any specific entry fee. Visitors are encouraged to take a photo with the sign and share it for a chance to receive a free t-shirt, though availability of the promotion should be confirmed on-site.

River Street Savannah, Georgia

Location: River St, Savannah, GA 31401, United States
Plus Code: 3WJ5+MV Savannah, Georgia, USA
Contact: +1 912-234-4608
Website: N/A

Opening Hours:
- **Monday to Friday:** 9:30 am – 9:30 pm
- **Saturday:** 9:30 am – 10:00 pm
- **Sunday:** 9:30 am – 9:30 pm
- **Closed on Public Holidays:** Hours might differ

Description: River Street is a historic waterfront thoroughfare in Savannah, Georgia, offering a vibrant mix of boutiques, restaurants, and scenic views of the Savannah River. The cobblestone streets and historic buildings contribute to the street's picturesque charm. Visitors can enjoy a range of dining options, from Southern comfort food to international cuisine. Street performers and local artisans enhance the lively atmosphere. The area features a riverfront park perfect for leisurely strolls, and there are markets with various local crafts and goods. River Street also provides views of large cargo ships and replica paddle steamers, showcasing Savannah's active port. While the street is a major tourist destination, it remains a significant spot for experiencing Savannah's unique character and historical appeal.

Nearby Attractions: The area along River Street offers excellent views of the Savannah River and the downtown skyline. Nearby attractions include the Savannah Riverfront Park and various historic sites throughout the city.

Important Information for Visitors: River Street is accessible year-round and is free to explore. The area can become crowded, especially during weekends and holidays, so it is advisable to plan visits accordingly. For dining and shopping, reservations might be necessary, particularly during peak times. The cobblestone streets and historic ambiance are significant highlights, but visitors should be aware of their surroundings and consider visiting during daylight hours for a more pleasant experience.

Lover's Oak

Location: 828 Albany St, Brunswick, GA 31520, United States
Plus Code: 4GR7+W9 Brunswick, Georgia, USA
Contact: N/A
Website: goldenisles.com
Opening Hours: Open 24 hours

Description: Lover's Oak is a historic live oak tree located in Brunswick, Georgia. This impressive tree, situated on an island in the middle of a residential street, is notable for its enormous size and age. It is a popular landmark, renowned for its historical significance and striking appearance. Visitors can admire the tree up close as it is easily accessible from the street, with no admission fee required. The surrounding area is predominantly residential, with limited street parking available. The tree's historical value is complemented by its dramatic presence, making it a noteworthy stop for those exploring Brunswick.

Nearby Attractions: While in Brunswick, visitors might also explore other significant landmarks and natural attractions in the area.

Important Information for Visitors: Lover's Oak is accessible at all hours, and no reservation is needed. It is recommended to visit during daylight for the best experience. As the tree is located on a small island within the street, be cautious of traffic and ensure safe viewing conditions.

Colonial Park Cemetery

Location: 200 Abercorn St, Savannah, GA 31401, United States
Plus Code: 3WG6+32 Savannah, Georgia, USA
Contact: +1 912-651-6843
Website: www.savannahga.gov
Opening Hours:
Monday to Sunday: 8 am – 8 pm
Description: Colonial Park Cemetery, located in the heart of Savannah's historic district, is a significant landmark with deep historical roots. Established in 1750, it served as the final resting place for numerous residents, including notable figures from the American Revolutionary War. Although closed to interments since 1853, visitors can still walk through this serene cemetery and explore the historic grave markers and monuments. The grounds are well-maintained by the city, but some of the older gravestones are in

disrepair, with several being difficult to read due to age. The cemetery's tranquil atmosphere offers a reflective experience, while historical signs and markers provide insight into the lives of those interred here. Colonial Park Cemetery is also a popular location for ghost tours, adding a mystical layer to its rich history.

Nearby Attractions: The cemetery is centrally located in Savannah's historic district, making it convenient for exploring nearby parks, museums, and iconic landmarks.

Important Information for Visitors: The cemetery is open daily from 8 am to 8 pm, with two main exit points. For a fuller experience, visiting during the late afternoon or evening can add a deeper appreciation of its history and atmosphere. No reservations are required, and the site is free to the public.

Cascade Springs Nature Preserve

Location: 2852 Cascade Rd, Atlanta, GA 30311, United States
Plus Code: PG99+RF Atlanta, Georgia, USA
Contact: +1 404-546-6744
Website: www.atlantatrails.com
Opening Hours:
Monday to Sunday: 8 am – 11 pm
Description: Cascade Springs Nature Preserve offers a refreshing escape from the urban environment of Atlanta, providing visitors with a serene and scenic retreat in dense woodlands. The preserve features well-worn nature trails along a picturesque river, ideal for smooth walks, while more challenging routes with rocky paths and exposed roots provide variety for hikers. The natural rock formations along the trails also make it a fun space for children to explore. The preserve includes picnic areas, though some tables are in disrepair. Wildlife such as deer is often spotted, enhancing the experience of being immersed in nature. Though the preserve offers multiple trail options, signage is limited, so it is important to be mindful of the various forks along the paths. The recently renovated parking lot provides easier access to the preserve.

Nearby Attractions: Located within Atlanta, the nature preserve is close to other parks and recreational areas, making it a convenient stop for those exploring the city's outdoor spaces.

Important Information for Visitors: The trails are open from 8 am to 11 pm daily, and entry is free. No reservations are needed, and the trails are dog-friendly, making it a popular spot for pet owners.

Center for Puppetry Arts

Location: 1404 Spring St NW, Atlanta, GA 30309, United States
Plus Code: QJV6+43 Atlanta, Georgia, USA
Contact: +1 404-873-3391
Website: www.puppet.org
Opening Hours:
Monday: Closed
Tuesday to Friday: 9 am – 5 pm
Saturday: 10 am – 5 pm
Sunday: 12 pm – 5 pm

Description: The Center for Puppetry Arts in Atlanta is a renowned institution dedicated to the art of puppetry, offering a delightful experience for both children and adults. It features an extensive collection of puppets, including a detailed Jim Henson exhibition showcasing iconic creations from "The Muppets" to "The Dark Crystal." Visitors can also explore international puppetry, with exhibits from Japan, England, and other cultures. The center hosts engaging puppet shows, workshops, and exhibits that cater to a range of interests. Free parking is available, and the center provides interactive areas, including workshops where children can create their own puppets. With its blend of history, nostalgia, and hands-on fun, this venue is a must-visit for puppet enthusiasts and those looking for a unique cultural experience. Admission is typically $16, with discounts for children and special events.

Nearby Attractions: The center is located in Midtown Atlanta, a short distance from attractions such as Piedmont Park and the High Museum of Art, making it a convenient cultural stop in the heart of the city.

Important Information for Visitors: It is recommended to check the schedule for puppet shows in advance, as the center offers a rotating selection of performances. The Jim Henson exhibition is a highlight, featuring many rare and historic puppets.

Rock Garden Calhoun

Location: 1411 Rome Rd SW, Calhoun, GA 30701, United States
Located in: Calhoun Seventh-day Adventist Church
Plus Code: F278+HC Calhoun, Georgia, USA
Contact: +1 706-629-5470
Website: www.calhounsdachurch.com
Opening Hours:
Monday to Sunday: 9 am – 7 pm
Hours may vary on holidays.

Description: The Rock Garden in Calhoun, Georgia, is a serene, art-filled attraction located behind the Calhoun Seventh-day Adventist Church. It features intricately designed stone castles, buildings, and whimsical sculptures that make the garden a hidden gem for visitors seeking a peaceful retreat. The garden showcases meticulous attention to detail, with miniature structures that include hidden figures inside windows and behind doors, inviting exploration and curiosity. In addition to the garden's artful displays, there are walking trails through the surrounding forest, offering a tranquil escape with scenic views. The main trail is a mile-long loop, providing a moderately challenging hike over the hill that backs the garden. Seating areas are scattered throughout for prayer, reflection, or simply enjoying the surroundings.

The garden is free to the public, with discreet donation boxes available for those who wish to contribute to its upkeep. The garden is well-maintained by the church and local community volunteers.

Important Information for Visitors:
Due to a previous incident, pets are no longer allowed. Bug spray is

recommended for the trail, and appropriate footwear is advised for hiking. The garden is easily accessible, with parking available in front and no long walking required to reach the entrance.

Nearby Attractions: The Rock Garden is located near Calhoun's downtown area, where additional dining and shopping options are available for visitors.

Georgia Nuclear Aircraft Laboratory

Location: Blue Trail, Dawsonville, GA 30534, United States
Plus Code: 9V24+F9 Dawsonville, Georgia, USA
Description: The Georgia Nuclear Aircraft Laboratory (GNAL) is a remnant of Cold War-era research located in Dawson Forest Wildlife Management Area. The laboratory was once used for testing the feasibility of nuclear-powered aircraft and included a blockhouse, which still stands today. The area is popular with hikers, mountain bikers, and horse riders for its network of trails winding through the dense forest. Though access to the blockhouse itself is prohibited and surrounded by barbed fencing, visitors can still walk the perimeter and observe the site from a distance.

The surrounding forest offers natural beauty but is less maintained than other recreational areas, adding to the site's eerie atmosphere. Some visitors report encountering muddy trails and an overall sense of mystery in the area. The Blue Trail, which leads to the blockhouse, is sometimes confusing due to limited signage.

While GNAL remains a fascinating site for history buffs and adventure seekers, caution is advised due to the area's occasional use for hunting and shooting activities.

Important Information for Visitors:
The blockhouse is off-limits, with security fencing around it. Visitors can walk around the perimeter, but access to the building itself is strictly prohibited. For safety, be aware of hunters in the area, particularly during hunting seasons.

Nearby Attractions: Dawson Forest Wildlife Management Area offers additional trails for hiking and biking, along with scenic spots for outdoor activities.

Braswell Mountain Rail Tunnel

Location: Silver Comet Trail, Rockmart, GA 30153, United States

Plus Code: X2FQ+46 Rockmart, Georgia, USA

Description: The Braswell Mountain Rail Tunnel is a historic highlight along the Silver Comet Trail, attracting cyclists, walkers, and history enthusiasts alike. This tunnel, originally built as part of a rail line, has since been integrated into the multi-use trail and offers a unique experience with its long, gently sloping pathway. The tunnel is well-lit and provides a cooler refuge on hot days, making it a popular stop for those seeking a break during their trek.

Stretching approximately 2.5 miles east of the Coots Lake trailhead, the path to the tunnel is lined with scenic views and resting areas, making it ideal for families and casual adventurers. However, visitors should be prepared for some muddy conditions, as water tends to collect inside the tunnel, especially after rain.

The acoustics of the tunnel add to its charm, with many enjoying the echoes as they pass through. For those traveling by bike, the smooth ride through the tunnel is often described as exhilarating.

Important Information for Visitors:

- Be aware that the tunnel may contain standing water after rain, making the path damp and potentially slippery.

- While the tunnel is generally safe and well-maintained, visitors should exercise caution, especially during inclement weather.

Trap Music Museum

Location: 630 Travis St NW, Atlanta, GA 30318, United States
Plus Code: QHCR+PH Atlanta, Georgia, USA
Website: trapmusicmuseum.us
Contact: Not publicly listed
Opening Hours:

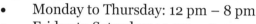

- Monday to Thursday: 12 pm – 8 pm
- Friday to Saturday: 12 pm – 9 pm
- Sunday: 12 pm – 8 pm

Description: The Trap Music Museum in Atlanta is a vibrant cultural experience that pays homage to the influential genre of trap music and its roots in Southern hip-hop culture. Showcasing exhibits that celebrate both the music and its impact on pop culture, the museum features a blend of artwork, memorabilia, and installations from iconic trap artists. A notable highlight is the immersive escape room experience that adds a layer of interaction to the museum's offerings.

Visitors praise the atmosphere and artistry but note that the museum experience is relatively brief, typically taking 30 minutes to complete. Weekends can be busy, with lines and wait times of up to 60 minutes, especially in the heat. The museum also offers a range of merchandise and refreshments inside, though parking costs around $20.

Important Information for Visitors:

- Reservations are recommended for weekends to avoid long waits.
- Expect to spend around 30 minutes inside, with ticket prices starting at $29.99.
- Parking is available for $20, and the museum offers merchandise and food on-site.

Waffle House Museum

Location: 2719 E College Ave, Decatur, GA 30030, United States
Plus Code: QPFC+RJ Decatur, Georgia, USA
Website: wafflehouse.com
Contact: +1 770-326-7086

Opening Hours:

- Open by appointment only. Check the website or call for scheduling.

Description: The Waffle House Museum in Decatur, Georgia, stands on the site of the original Waffle House, opened in 1955. This nostalgic museum offers visitors a peek into American dining history, showcasing exhibits such as original uniforms, menus from different decades, and a restored 1950s diner setting. For those passionate about this iconic Southern chain, the museum provides an engaging, family-friendly experience.

On free weekends, visitors can enjoy complimentary waffles and Coca-Cola. While the museum is not an operating restaurant, it offers a unique experience, making it a must-visit for Waffle House fans. Reservations are recommended as the museum is not open daily, and special events often fill up quickly.

Important Information for Visitors:
- Reservations are required for tours, and the museum is open only on select days or by appointment.
- The museum is not a functioning restaurant, so don't expect food unless it's a special event weekend.
- Parking is available, and tours are free.

Folk Art Park

Location: Courtland St NE, Atlanta, GA 30308, United States
Plus Code: QJ78+J9 Atlanta, Georgia, USA
Opening Hours: Monday to Sunday: 6 am – 11 pm

Description: Folk Art Park, located in the heart of downtown Atlanta, offers a unique glimpse into Southern folk art, displayed across multiple small sections. This urban outdoor exhibit showcases colorful murals and art installations created by self-taught local artists, reflecting Georgia's rich cultural heritage. The park's proximity to the interstate and heavy traffic can make it difficult to access, and visitors should be aware of the surrounding environment, especially at night.

While it provides an interesting spot to take a break and appreciate local art, the park is small and can feel underwhelming to some visitors. Families may find it more engaging during warmer months when kids are skateboarding nearby, though the lack of amenities such as restrooms and seating can be a drawback.

Important Information for Visitors:
- Parking can be challenging, and the park is situated near heavy traffic areas.
- No restrooms or designated seating available.
- The surrounding area may feel unsafe to some, especially at night. Use caution when visiting.

Nearby Attractions:
- Atlanta Civic Center
- The Varsity

Pin Point Heritage Museum

Location: 9924 Pin Point Ave, Savannah, GA 31406, United States
Plus Code: XW25+VV Savannah, Georgia, USA
Contact: +1 912-355-0064
Website: www.chsgeorgia.org

Opening Hours:
- Thursday to Friday: 9am – 4pm
- Saturday: 9am – 4pm
- Closed on Sunday, Monday, Tuesday, and Wednesday

Description: The Pin Point Heritage Museum, located on the original site of the historic Gullah/Geechee community, offers an immersive look into the lives and culture of this resourceful community. The museum features exhibits that highlight the local history, including a detailed documentary about the area's rich heritage. Visitors can explore displays on the oyster shucking and canning industry, and enjoy views of the surrounding marshlands. The museum provides an opportunity to learn about the Gullah/Geechee culture through well-organized exhibits and passionate staff.

Nearby Attractions:

- **Old Fort Jackson:** A historic fortification located nearby, offering tours and educational programs on Savannah's military history.

- **Savannah History Museum:** Located in the historic district, this museum provides additional context on Savannah's past.

Important Information for Visitors:

- The museum is part of the Coastal Heritage Society's ticket package, offering discounted admission to multiple museums.

- The last guided tour typically ends around 2pm, so it's advisable to arrive earlier if interested in the guided experience.

- Entry fees are $11–15 for adults.

Videodrome

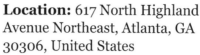

Location: 617 North Highland Avenue Northeast, Atlanta, GA 30306, United States
Plus Code: QJCX+F4 Atlanta, Georgia, USA
Contact: +1 404-885-1117
Website: www.videodromeatl.com
Opening Hours: Monday to Sunday: 12pm – 10pm
Description: Videodrome is a specialty rental store for movie enthusiasts, offering a diverse collection of obscure and independent films on modern formats such as Blu-ray and 4K. The store caters to those seeking rare and unique titles, though it does include some adult-themed content, which may not be suitable for all visitors. Rentals are priced at $5 for a 10-day period. The store is recognized for its extensive movie library and knowledgeable staff, who are passionate about cinema. Note that parking is available on-site but is limited and can be tight.

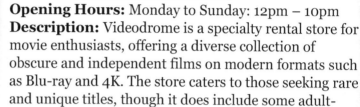

Nearby Attractions:
- **The Fox Theatre:** A historic theater offering a variety of live performances and classic films.
- **Ponce City Market:** A mixed-use development featuring shops, dining, and entertainment options.

Important Information for Visitors:
- The store is popular among movie buffs and provides a curated selection of films. If you have specific interests in independent or hard-to-find movies, this is a worthwhile stop.
- Limited parking may require some patience, so plan accordingly.

Hindu Temple of Atlanta

Location: 5851 GA-85, Riverdale, GA 30274, United States
Plus Code: HHWR+5H Riverdale, Georgia, USA
Contact: +1 770-907-7102
Website: www.hindutempleofatlanta.org

Opening Hours:

- Monday to Sunday: 9am – 9pm

Description: The Hindu Temple of Atlanta is the oldest Hindu temple in the area and a significant center for the local Hindu community. It features various Hindu deities, including temples dedicated to Venkateswara and Shiva. The temple's architecture is noted for its beauty, and it is home to a Pipal and Vata Vriksha tree. The temple organizes events according to the Hindu calendar, including monthly Poojas. It also offers amenities such as a canteen with reasonably priced prasad, a conference hall, and an outdoor stage for events. It is recommended for those seeking spiritual solace, blessings, and community connection.

Nearby Attractions:

- **Atlanta Motor Speedway:** A major racing venue offering events and tours.

- **Chattahoochee Hills:** A scenic area ideal for outdoor activities.

Important Information for Visitors:

- Visitors are expected to remove their shoes before entering the temple and to respect the customs of the space. Photography is generally not permitted inside the temple.

- The temple provides facilities for various Poojas and ceremonies, and catering services are available for events held on the premises.

Robert C. Williams Paper Museum

Location: 500 10th St NW, Atlanta, GA 30332, United States
Plus Code: QHJW+95 Atlanta, Georgia, USA
Contact: +1 404-894-6663
Website: www.paper.gatech.edu

Opening Hours: 9am – 5pm
- Saturday: Closed
- Sunday: Closed

Description: The Robert C. Williams Paper Museum, located on the Georgia Institute of Technology campus, is a unique institution dedicated to the history and technology of paper making. It features a range of permanent exhibits showcasing the evolution of paper from ancient papyrus to modern mills, including artifacts, machinery, and materials. The museum also highlights innovative paper-making techniques and the environmental aspects of recycling. Entry is free, though donations are encouraged. It is an excellent educational resource, particularly for school groups interested in learning about the paper industry and recycling processes.

Nearby Attractions:
- **Georgia Aquarium:** One of the largest aquariums in the world, offering a variety of marine exhibits.
- **World of Coca-Cola:** A museum dedicated to the history of the Coca-Cola Company and its iconic beverage.

Important Information for Visitors:
- The museum is part of the Georgia Institute of Technology and is located within the campus.
- While there is no admission fee, visitors are encouraged to contribute to the donation box.
- The museum may have limited hours or be closed on some holidays, so checking the schedule before visiting is advisable.

Wat Lao Buddha Phothisaram

Location: 4443 E Conley Rd, Conley, GA 30288, United States
Plus Code: MM2G+8M Conley, Georgia, USA
Contact: +1 404-361-7805
Website: www.facebook.com (Official updates may be found here)
Opening Hours:
- Monday to Sunday: 10am – 6pm

Description: Wat Lao Buddha Phothisaram is a serene and culturally rich Buddhist temple located in Conley, Georgia. The temple features traditional Lao architecture with intricate details that reflect its cultural heritage. Visitors can experience a peaceful environment conducive to meditation and spiritual reflection. The temple is open daily and welcomes donations to support its upkeep and restoration efforts. However, the temple's administration occasionally faces challenges in maintaining the facility, including overgrown grass and uneven entry roads, which may affect the overall visitor experience. Despite these issues, the temple provides a tranquil space for spiritual enrichment and a glimpse into Lao Buddhist practices.

Nearby Attractions:
- **Panola Mountain State Park:** Offers hiking trails and nature walks through scenic landscapes.
- **Atlanta Botanical Garden:** A renowned garden showcasing diverse plant collections and seasonal displays.

Important Information for Visitors:
- It is recommended to confirm the temple's open status before visiting, as maintenance or renovation work may affect accessibility.
- Donations are appreciated to aid in the temple's restoration and maintenance.
- Parking is available, but be aware of potential road conditions leading to the temple.

Lake Claire Community Land Trust

Location: 270 Arizona Ave NE, Atlanta, GA 30307, United States
Plus Code: QM69+MQ Atlanta, Georgia, USA
Website: www.lcclt.org

Opening Hours:
- Monday to Sunday: 8am – 8pm

Description: The Lake Claire Community Land Trust (LCCLT) is a community-managed green space located in the heart of Atlanta. This urban oasis is designed to be a self-sustaining environment featuring rain barrels, a community garden, and meditation areas. It is home to a variety of plants and flowers, a playground, and a unique attraction—a resident emu named Big Lou, who resides near a turtle pond. The land trust serves as a venue for community events, including drum circles held on the first Saturday of each month. Visitors can enjoy a quiet stroll, a picnic, or simply explore the tranquil setting. Donations are welcomed to support the upkeep of the garden and the welfare of the animals.

Nearby Attractions:
- **Atlanta Botanical Garden:** Offers expansive gardens and seasonal exhibitions.
- **Piedmont Park:** A large urban park with walking trails, sports fields, and events.

Important Information for Visitors:
- The land trust is open daily, but specific activities or events may vary, so checking the website for current information is recommended.
- Donations are encouraged to support the garden's maintenance and the care of resident animals.
- Leashed pets are welcome, and visitors should respect the space and its community guidelines.

St. Marys Submarine Museum

Location: 102 St Marys St W, St Marys, GA 31558, United States
Plus Code: PFC2+68 St Marys, Georgia, USA
Contact: +1 912-882-2782
Website:
www.stmaryssubmuseum.com

Opening Hours:
- Monday: Closed
- Tuesday to Friday: 10am – 5pm
- Saturday: 10am – 5pm
- Sunday: Closed

Description: The St. Marys Submarine Museum offers an in-depth look at the history and technology of the US Submarine Force. Located on St Marys Street, this museum showcases a range of artifacts and exhibits related to underwater warfare. Visitors can explore two floors of displays, including early submarine memorabilia, a functional periscope, and modern submarine artifacts. The museum features informative exhibits on submarine technology and its role in various conflicts, as well as a short film detailing life aboard submarines. A gift shop is located on the lower floor. Entry fees range from $6 to $10, and the museum provides a unique educational experience for those interested in naval history.

Nearby Attractions:
- **Cumberland Island National Seashore:** A beautiful barrier island with pristine beaches and historic sites.
- **St. Marys Historic District:** Offers charming shops and historic buildings.

Important Information for Visitors:
- The museum is closed on Sundays and Mondays, and operates with limited hours on Saturdays.
- It is recommended to check the website for any changes in hours or special events.
- There is a small fee for entry, and donations are appreciated to support museum operations.

Plant Riverside

Location: 500 W River St, Savannah, GA 31401, United States
Plus Code: 3WM3+GF Savannah, Georgia, USA
Contact: +1 912-644-6400
Website: www.savannahga.gov
Opening Hours:

- Monday to Sunday: 24 hours (parking garage hours may vary)

Description: Plant Riverside is a vibrant mixed-use development located on the Savannah Riverfront. It features a blend of dining, entertainment, and retail options, along with stunning views of the river. The complex includes a variety of restaurants, shops, and spaces for live music and events. It serves as a lively hub for visitors exploring Savannah's historic district, offering convenient access to both cultural attractions and scenic river views. The area is ideal for both day and night visits, with options for outdoor and indoor activities.

Nearby Attractions:

- **Savannah Historic District:** A well-preserved area featuring historic homes, squares, and landmarks.

- **Forsyth Park:** A large park known for its iconic fountain and beautiful gardens.

Important Information for Visitors:

- Parking can be challenging, particularly on weekends. The parking garage has limited space and may have accessibility issues.

- It is recommended to use rideshare services or public transportation for easier access, especially during peak times.

- The area can be crowded during events and weekends, so plan accordingly.

Computer Museum of America

Location: 5000 Commerce Pkwy, Roswell, GA 30076, United States
Plus Code: 2MQ5+FV Roswell, Georgia, USA
Contact: +1 770-695-0651

Website: www.computermuseumofamerica.org
Opening Hours:
- Saturday: 10 am–5 pm
- Sunday: 12–5 pm
- Monday (Labor Day): Closed
- Tuesday: Closed
- Wednesday: Closed
- Thursday: 12–5 pm
- Friday: 12–5 pm

Description: The Computer Museum of America offers an extensive exploration of computing history, featuring exhibits on the evolution of technology from early computers to modern advancements. The museum showcases a variety of artifacts, including vintage computers, arcade games, and space technology. Highlights include displays of the Apollo flight computers, an Enigma machine, and retro gaming consoles. The museum is located near Roswell Town Center, making it convenient for visitors to enjoy other local attractions.

Nearby Attractions:

- **Roswell Town Center:** A shopping and entertainment area with dining and leisure options.

- **Chattahoochee Nature Center:** Offers outdoor activities and educational programs about local wildlife and nature.

Important Information for Visitors:

- Reservations are recommended, especially for group visits or corporate events.

- The museum may have limited staffing and exhibit updates; check the website or call ahead for the latest information.

- The area has ample parking, and the museum is located close to additional amenities such as a movie theater and mini golf.

Fort Mountain Rock Fort

Location: Chatsworth, GA 30705, United States
Plus Code: Q7JR+C7 Chatsworth, Georgia, USA
Opening Hours: 6 am–10 pm
Description: Fort Mountain Rock Fort is a historic site featuring an ancient rock wall located atop Fort Mountain. The area is known for its scenic trails, including a path leading to a fire tower and a

breathtaking overlook. The trail is moderately challenging, with stone steps and forest paths, and is best navigated with appropriate footwear. The site includes restrooms and parking at the trailhead. The park is well-maintained, offering a mix of history and natural beauty.

Nearby Attractions:

- **Fort Mountain State Park:** Offers additional hiking trails and camping facilities.
- **Cohutta Wilderness Area:** Known for its extensive backcountry trails and natural scenery.

Important Information for Visitors:

- Admission fee ranges from $1 to $5.
- The trail is not ADA accessible; suitable footwear is recommended.
- Restrooms are available at the parking lot.

Howard Finster's Paradise Gardens

Location: 200 N Lewis St, Summerville, GA 30747, United States
Plus Code: GM7M+5F Summerville, Georgia, USA
Opening Hours: 11 am–5 pm

Description: Howard Finster's Paradise Gardens is a vibrant folk art environment created by renowned artist Howard Finster. The site features a diverse array of 2D and 3D artworks, including buildings and installations scattered throughout the grounds. Visitors can explore Finster's workshops and collections, showcasing his eclectic artistic vision and religious themes. The gardens offer a unique glimpse into Finster's artistic process and personal history. The self-guided tour allows for exploration of art both indoors and outdoors, including intriguing pieces set in the landscape.

Nearby Attractions:

- **Summerville's Historic District:** Offers additional historical and cultural sites.

- **James H. (Sloppy) Floyd Park:** Provides outdoor recreational opportunities and scenic views.

Important Information for Visitors:

- Admission fee ranges from $6 to $10.

- The site includes a paved path, but some areas may be challenging for those with mobility issues.

- Check the official website for updates on facility availability and any potential changes to the opening hours.

Atlanta Botanical Garden

Location: 1345 Piedmont Ave NE, Atlanta, GA 30309, United States
Plus Code: QJQG+XX Atlanta, Georgia, USA
Opening Hours: 9 am–9 pm
Description: The Atlanta Botanical Garden offers a stunning array of plant displays and themed exhibits. The garden features lush greenery, intricate floral designs, and engaging installations such as the current Alice in Wonderland theme. Key attractions include the Earth Goddess, the canopy walk, and various themed greenhouses. The garden is well-

maintained with diverse plant collections and engaging features for all ages, including interactive exhibits for children and opportunities for photography.

Nearby Attractions:

- **Piedmont Park:** A large urban park offering walking trails, sports fields, and scenic views.

- **Atlanta History Center:** Provides exhibits on the history of Atlanta and Southern history.

Important Information for Visitors:

- Admission prices are generally higher during special exhibits.

- Parking is available, but it can be crowded; consider walking if you're nearby.

- The garden offers military discounts and has facilities for dining and refreshments.

- Reentry is allowed only within 15 minutes of departure.

- It is recommended to wear comfortable shoes and bring water, especially during hot weather.

Battle of Atlanta Cyclorama

Location: 130 W Paces Ferry Rd NW, Atlanta, GA 30305, United States
Plus Code: RJR7+HR Atlanta, Georgia, USA
Opening Hours: 9 am–4 pm
Description: The Battle of Atlanta Cyclorama, located within the Atlanta History Center, showcases an impressive 19th-century panoramic painting depicting the Civil War battle. The cylindrical viewing area allows for a 360-degree view of the massive artwork. Visitors can ascend to a higher platform via escalator for a better vantage point. The exhibit includes a 10-minute introductory film and interactive displays providing context about the painting and its historical significance. The

detailed artwork captures both the foreground and background intricately, offering a deep dive into this pivotal moment in history.

Nearby Attractions:

- **Atlanta History Center:** Home to the Cyclorama, the center also features historic houses, gardens, and additional exhibits on Southern history.

- **Piedmont Park:** Nearby park offering recreational facilities and scenic views.

Important Information for Visitors:

- Comfortable shoes are recommended due to the museum's extensive exhibits.

- Allow ample time to explore, as there is a lot to see and learn.

- Tickets range from $16 to $20 for adults.

- Reservations are recommended, especially on weekends.

Gravity Research Foundation Monument

Location: 400 Dowman Dr, Atlanta, GA 30322, United States

Plus Code: QMRF+26 Atlanta, Georgia, USA

Description: The Gravity Research Foundation Monument, situated on the campus of Emory University, is a historical plaque established by Roger Babson, the founder of the Gravity Research Foundation. Founded in 1948, the organization aims to explore ways to block or control gravity. The monument is one of 15 similar plaques installed across the East Coast, reflecting Babson's interest in promoting scientific research into gravity. The Foundation continues to host an annual essay competition with prizes of up to $4,000, encouraging ongoing research into the phenomenon of gravitation.

While the monument itself may not be a major attraction, it represents a unique piece of scientific curiosity and history. The story behind the Foundation and its continued relevance in the study of gravity adds an interesting layer to this small but notable plaque.

Nearby Attractions:

- **Emory University Campus:** Explore the campus grounds, which offer a mix of historical and contemporary architectural styles.

- **Fernbank Museum of Natural History:** Located nearby, this museum offers extensive exhibits on natural history and science.

Important Information for Visitors:

- The monument is accessible on foot within the Emory University campus.

- It may be of particular interest to those with a fascination for science and history.

HOTEL

Hilton Garden Inn Atlanta North/Alpharetta

Location: 4025 Windward Plaza, Alpharetta, GA 30005, United States
Plus Code: 3QR6+X6 Alpharetta, Georgia, USA
Contact: +1 770-360-7766
Website: www.hilton.com
Check-in time: 15:00
Check-out time: 12:00
Description: Hilton Garden Inn Atlanta North/Alpharetta offers a convenient location near office buildings and dining options. The hotel features a clean and quiet environment, ideal for business travelers. Rooms are equipped with basic amenities, but some guests have reported issues with the A/C unit cycling on and off, which may affect sleep quality. The

property includes a pool and other common areas, though maintenance may vary. Guests can find nearby dining options, including Indian food and Mellow Mushroom, though experiences may vary. The hotel does not offer complimentary breakfast, but a Starbucks is a short drive away.

Nearby Attractions: The hotel is situated close to various office buildings and restaurants, making it suitable for business trips.

Country Inn & Suites by Radisson, Tifton, GA

Location: 310 S Virginia Ave, Tifton, GA 31794, United States

Plus Code: FF2C+J9 Tifton, Georgia, USA

Contact: +1 229-256-4488

Website: www.choicehotels.com

Check-in time: 14:00

Check-out time: 12:00

  Description: Country Inn & Suites by Radisson in Tifton, Georgia, offers a convenient location right off I-75, making it an excellent stop for travelers. The hotel provides clean, spacious rooms with comfortable beds and pillows, ensuring a restful stay. The property features an indoor pool and workout room, and offers a varied complimentary breakfast. Highway noise is minimal, although a distant train may be heard at night. The front desk staff is noted for being helpful and professional, even in challenging situations. While the hotel meets the needs of families and solo travelers alike, some amenities, like the small coffee maker, could be improved. Overall, the hotel offers good value and comfort for its price range.

Nearby Attractions: The hotel is located near I-75, making it a convenient stopover for road travelers. There are various dining options and shops in the vicinity for added convenience.

Comfort Inn & Suites

Location: 320 S Virginia Ave, Tifton, GA 31794, United States
Plus Code: FF2C+G4 Tifton, Georgia, USA
Contact: +1 229-375-5903
Website: www.choicehotels.com
Check-in time: 15:00
Check-out time: 11:00
Description: Comfort Inn & Suites in Tifton, Georgia, is an excellent option for road travelers looking for comfort and value. The hotel provides spacious, clean rooms with well-maintained amenities, including cold refrigerators, functional microwaves, and effective air conditioning. The staff is highly praised for their hospitality, offering a warm and welcoming experience that makes guests feel at home. Maintenance and housekeeping are prompt and efficient, ensuring everything runs smoothly. The property includes a well-maintained pool, and the complimentary breakfast features a range of options, including crispy bacon. LGBTQ+ friendly and family-oriented, this hotel offers great value for the money and is a popular choice for travelers heading to Florida.

Nearby Attractions: The hotel is conveniently located off I-75, making it an ideal stopover for travelers. Local dining options and shops are available in the nearby vicinity.

Super 8 by Wyndham Adel

Location: 1103 W 4th St, Adel, GA 31620, United States
Plus Code: 4HM7+G4 Adel, Georgia, USA
Contact: +1 229-513-1019
Website: www.wyndhamhotels.com

Check-in time: 15:00
Check-out time: 11:00
 Description: Super 8 by Wyndham Adel offers budget accommodations for travelers in Adel, Georgia. While the hotel welcomes pets for an additional fee, guests have experienced mixed results regarding cleanliness and room conditions. Some rooms, especially those previously used as smoking rooms, retain unpleasant odors and may trigger asthma symptoms. Housekeeping issues, such as unclean carpets and bathrooms, have been noted. Despite this, the staff is often praised for their friendliness and effort to address guest concerns. The pool is well-maintained, and complimentary breakfast is available, though offerings are basic. The hotel may suit travelers seeking an economical stop, but guests should be prepared for potential issues with room cleanliness.

Nearby Attractions: Located just off I-75, Super 8 by Wyndham Adel provides easy access for road travelers. Several local dining options and shops are available in the area.

Best Western Acworth Inn

Location: 5155 Cowan Rd, Acworth, GA 30101, United States
Plus Code: 38GW+V4 Acworth, Georgia, USA
Contact: +1 770-974-0116
Website: www.bestwestern.com
Check-in time: 14:00
Check-out time: 11:00

 Description: Best Western Acworth Inn is an economical option for travelers passing through or staying in Acworth, Georgia. Situated just off I-75, it offers convenient access to both Atlanta and the charming nearby town of Marietta. The hotel is known for its friendly staff and clean rooms, which come equipped with modern amenities such as mini-fridges, microwaves, and irons. Guests can enjoy a complimentary breakfast that includes a variety of options such as eggs, biscuits, sausage, cereals, and fresh fruit. The hotel's outdoor pool is well-maintained, though it may occasionally be closed for maintenance. Renovations are ongoing, with updates to carpets and fixtures in the rooms, and future upgrades are planned, including new furniture and larger TVs. The hotel is pet-friendly and has a grassy area suitable for dogs. Walking distance from fast food outlets like McDonald's and a short drive from more diverse dining and shopping options, the location is ideal for both leisure and business travelers.

Nearby Attractions: Marietta Square, Lake Acworth, Kennesaw Mountain National Battlefield Park, and downtown Atlanta's popular attractions, including the Georgia Aquarium and Centennial Olympic Park, are within easy reach by car.

Days Inn by Wyndham Kingsland GA

Location: 1353 GA-40, Kingsland, GA 31548, United States
Plus Code: Q8RW+6C Kingsland, Georgia, USA
Contact: +1 912-330-6444
Website: www.wyndhamhotels.com
Check-in time: 15:00
Check-out time: 11:00
Description: Located just off I-95, Days Inn by Wyndham Kingsland is a budget-friendly option for travelers heading to or from Florida. The hotel offers basic accommodations, with rooms equipped with essentials like mini-fridges, microwaves, and flat-screen TVs. While the beds and pillows are generally comfortable, there have been mixed reviews about room cleanliness and maintenance, with some guests noting issues such as humidity, worn floors, and unpleasant odors in bathrooms. The complimentary breakfast includes limited options like waffles, cereal, and yogurt, but does not offer eggs or hot items like sausage. Pet owners are welcome, although some guests have noted insufficient replenishment of dog waste bags. The hotel features a small outdoor pool, and certain rooms provide poolside views.

Nearby Attractions: Cumberland Island National Seashore, Crooked River State Park, and St. Marys Submarine Museum are within a short driving distance.

Baymont by Wyndham Hinesville Fort Stewart Area

Location: 773 Veterans Pkwy, Hinesville, GA 31313, United States
Plus Code: R9MM+42 Hinesville, Georgia, USA
Contact: +1 912-408-4444
Website: www.wyndhamhotels.com
Check-in time: 14:00
Check-out time: 11:00
Description: Situated near Fort Stewart, Baymont by Wyndham Hinesville offers budget accommodations with mixed reviews. Some guests found the rooms spacious, clean, and comfortable, with friendly staff enhancing the overall experience. However, several visitors reported significant maintenance and cleanliness issues, including humidity problems, sticky floors, and unpleasant odors, which led to uncomfortable stays. The hotel is undergoing some renovations, including repairs to the pool, but many areas still require attention. Breakfast offerings are basic, with limited options. Despite these drawbacks, the location is convenient for those visiting Fort Stewart or the surrounding area.

Nearby Attractions: Fort Stewart Military Base, Liberty County Regional Park, and the Midway Museum.

Days Inn by Wyndham Blakely

Location: 1097 Arlington Ave, Blakely, GA 39823, United States
Plus Code: 93MG+PV Blakely, Georgia, USA
Contact: +1 229-723-5858

Website: www.wyndhamhotels.com
Check-in time: 15:00
Check-out time: 11:00
 Description: Days Inn by Wyndham Blakely offers basic accommodations with mixed feedback. Some guests appreciated the cleanliness, comfort, and friendly service provided by the staff. The location is convenient for those visiting family or passing through Blakely, and the property offers decent value for budget travelers. Breakfast is provided but is relatively simple. However, there have been reports of cleanliness issues, including pests, stained linens, and maintenance concerns such as missing smoke detectors. The air conditioning works, but some guests noted that it struggled to keep the rooms cool. Despite the challenges, it remains one of the few lodging options in Blakely and provides a satisfactory stay for many, especially when managed expectations for the price.

Nearby Attractions: Kolomoki Mounds State Park, Blakely's Town Square, and Early County Museum.

Hampton Inn Blue Ridge

Location: 50 W Main St, Blue Ridge, GA 30513, United States
Plus Code: VM9G+7Q Blue Ridge, Georgia, USA
Contact: +1 706-642-9001
Website: www.hilton.com
Check-in time: 16:00
Check-out time: 11:00

Description: Hampton Inn Blue Ridge is a centrally located hotel offering great convenience for travelers exploring downtown Blue Ridge, with easy access to shopping, dining, and the Scenic Railway just outside the front door. The hotel provides comfortable accommodations with clean, modern rooms and friendly service. Notable features include a rooftop restaurant offering good food and pleasant views, adding a unique touch to the experience.

While most guests appreciate the excellent location, clean facilities, and helpful staff, some noted shortcomings, including housekeeping policies where rooms are only refreshed every other day, and issues with humidity or cleanliness in some rooms. Breakfast is standard fare and satisfactory, though parking can be cramped, with an added $5.00 per night charge. Despite a few drawbacks, the overall feedback is positive, particularly regarding the ambiance and hospitality.

Nearby Attractions: Blue Ridge Scenic Railway, Blue Ridge City Park, Downtown Blue Ridge

Super 8 by Wyndham Ashburn

Location: 749 E Washington Ave, Ashburn, GA 31714, United States
Plus Code: P965+GR Ashburn, Georgia, USA
Contact: +1 229-329-1981
Website: www.wyndhamhotels.com
Check-in time: 02:00
Check-out time: 11:00
Description: Super 8 by Wyndham Ashburn offers budget-friendly accommodations, ideal for travelers looking for basic amenities at a reasonable price. The rooms are clean and seem to have been recently updated, providing comfortable beds and functional TVs. The breakfast is limited, offering waffles, cereal, and bagels, but sufficient for those not seeking a full continental spread. While the property is praised for its value, some guests have raised concerns about customer service, with a few encounters described as unfriendly or dismissive.

The Wi-Fi can be unreliable, and the hotel's cleanliness and atmosphere, while decent, may not meet higher expectations. However, for those traveling on a budget, the hotel offers a satisfactory stay at a low cost.

Nearby Attractions: Crime and Punishment Museum, Downtown Ashburn, Turner County Civic Center.

Holiday Inn Express & Suites Vidalia, an IHG Hotel

Location: 200 Michael Collins Dr, Vidalia, GA 30474, United States
Plus Code: 6J3H+XQ Vidalia, Georgia, USA
Contact: +1 912-403-3308
Website: www.ihg.com

Check-in time: 15:00
Check-out time: 11:00

Description: Holiday Inn Express & Suites Vidalia offers a modern and comfortable stay, maintaining IHG's well-known standards of service and amenities. Situated in a tranquil location, the hotel offers picturesque views of a nearby lake and surrounding fields, providing a peaceful atmosphere for guests. The hotel features clean, well-maintained rooms equipped with fast-cooling air conditioning, offering a great respite after a long day. Amenities include a well-kept pool, fitness center, and business services like computers for guest use.

The staff is highly regarded for their warmth and hospitality, always greeting guests with smiles and ensuring an efficient check-in process. Complimentary breakfast offers standard options, satisfying guests with quality and convenience. Though parking can be a challenge during busy periods, especially when large vehicles take up several spots, the hotel's quiet atmosphere and cleanliness make it a popular choice for travelers seeking comfort and value.

Nearby Attractions: Vidalia Onion Museum, Ladson Genealogical Library, and Hawk's Point Golf Club.

Important Information for Visitors: Quiet hours are observed after 9pm, ensuring a peaceful environment for all guests.

Hilton Garden Inn Atlanta Perimeter Center

Location: 1501 Lake Hearn Dr NE, Atlanta, GA 30319, United States
Plus Code: WM86+H7 Atlanta, Georgia, USA
Contact: +1 404-459-0500
Website: www.hilton.com

Check-in time: 16:00
Check-out time: 11:00

Description: Hilton Garden Inn Atlanta Perimeter Center is a hotel that caters to both business and leisure travelers. The hotel features a range of amenities including meeting spaces and an on-site restaurant. However, recent feedback indicates areas for improvement. Some guests have noted that the property feels dated and may not meet the cleanliness and service standards expected from the Hilton brand.

Issues reported include difficulties with room doors, inconsistent room temperatures, and unclean meeting facilities. Additionally, some guests have expressed dissatisfaction with the breakfast service and management's handling of breakfast hours. On a positive note, staff members like April have been praised for their helpfulness and professionalism.

The hotel provides a quiet environment and is conveniently located about 30 minutes north of the airport, making it a viable option for those needing proximity to the Perimeter area.

Nearby Attractions: Perimeter Mall, Dunwoody Nature Center, and Chattahoochee River National Recreation Area.

Important Information for Visitors: Guests should be aware that there have been issues reported with the breakfast service, including early closure and lack of signage. Additionally, some room amenities and common areas may require attention and maintenance.

By George Restaurant and Bar

Location:
127 Peachtree Rd NE, Floor 1, The Candler Building, Atlanta, GA 30303, United States
Plus Code: QJ46+QW Atlanta, Georgia, USA
Contact: +1 470-851-2752
Website: bygeorgeatl.com
Opening Hours: 7am – 10pm
Description: By George

Restaurant and Bar, located in the historic Candler Building, offers a stylish dining experience with a diverse menu that includes breakfast, lunch, and dinner options. The restaurant is known for its modern elegance and high-quality meals. For breakfast, patrons can enjoy a selection of well-prepared dishes such as avocado toast and cappuccino. For lunch and dinner, the menu features a range of options including seafood and meat dishes. A valet parking service is available for $6.00, which is added to the bill. The restaurant offers a pleasant dining atmosphere suitable for both casual meals and special occasions.
Nearby Attractions:

- **Candler Building**: A historical landmark with notable architecture and history.

The Dillard House Restaurant

Location:
768 Franklin St, Dillard, GA 30537, United States
Plus Code: XJ88+MG Dillard, Georgia, USA

Contact: +1 706-746-5348
Website: dillardhouse.com
Opening Hours:
Monday to Sunday: 7am – 8pm
Description: The Dillard House Restaurant, located in Dillard, Georgia, is known for its hearty Southern-style meals served family-style. With generous portions and a variety of dishes, this restaurant offers traditional Southern comfort foods such as country-fried steak, mashed potatoes, fried okra, and a variety of vegetables. The service is warm and attentive, ensuring that guests feel welcome and well taken care of during their meal. While the restaurant carries a nostalgic charm, some areas show signs of aging, which could benefit from updates. Despite this, the Dillard House remains a popular spot for both locals and tourists seeking a satisfying meal. Ample free parking is available on-site for visitors' convenience.

Nearby Attractions:

- **Dillard House Stables**: Enjoy horseback riding with scenic views of the North Georgia Mountains.

- **Black Rock Mountain State Park**: A popular destination for hiking and outdoor activities, located a short drive away.

Boar's Head Grill & Tavern

Location:
1 Lincoln St, Savannah, GA 31401, United States
Plus Code: 3WJ6+7V Savannah, Georgia, USA
Contact: +1 912-651-9660
Website: boarsheadgrill.com
Opening Hours:
Monday to Sunday: 11am – 10pm

Description: Boar's Head Grill & Tavern, located along the historic River Street in Savannah, offers a welcoming dining experience with a blend of old-world charm. This restaurant features a variety of dishes, including seafood, steaks, and Southern specialties such as the popular she crab soup. The atmosphere is cozy and reflective of Savannah's rich history, making it a fitting destination for both tourists and locals. The steaks are expertly prepared, while other popular menu items include bacon-wrapped shrimp and the warm chocolate bread pudding. The restaurant offers paid street parking, which can be challenging to find in the area, but it remains a standout dining spot away from the typical tourist traps.

Nearby Attractions:

- **River Street:** A historic street known for its shops, galleries, and scenic views of the Savannah River.

- **Savannah Historic District:** Just steps away, visitors can explore one of the largest National Historic Landmark Districts in the U.S.

Sea Salt Seafood Howell Mill

Location:
1801 Howell Mill Rd NW #400, Atlanta, GA 30318, United States
Located in: The District at Howell Mill
Plus Code: RH3P+7W Atlanta, Georgia, USA
Contact: +1 404-855-5800
Website: seasalthowellmill.com
Opening Hours:
Open daily until 2:30am
Description:
Sea Salt Seafood Howell Mill offers a vibrant dining atmosphere with a variety of seafood and Southern-style dishes in a lively setting. Known for dishes like Rasta Pasta

and catfish fingers, the restaurant blends excellent food with a fun ambiance. The service is attentive, and the menu includes seafood specialties such as lobster rolls and salmon burgers, as well as lighter options like fish and chips. The location also features karaoke after 9pm, making it a great spot for an energetic night out. While parking can be scarce due to its location within a busy shopping district, there are ample spaces available in nearby lots.

Nearby Attractions:

- **Atlantic Station:** Shopping and entertainment hub nearby.

- **The Works:** Popular mixed-use development with restaurants and entertainment.

Important Information for Visitors:
Plan to arrive early for better parking, and note that there is a 90-minute time limit for tables during peak times.

Indigo Coastal Shanty

Location: 1402 Reynolds St, Brunswick, GA 31520, United States
Plus Code: 4GX4+7G
Brunswick, Georgia, USA
Contact: +1 912-265-2007
Website:
indigocoastalshanty.com

Opening Hours:
- Saturday: 4pm – 9:30pm
- Sunday: Closed
- Monday (Labor Day): 11am – 3pm
- Tuesday to Thursday: 11am – 9pm
- Friday: 11am – 9:30pm

Description: Indigo Coastal Shanty is a cozy, laid-back eatery offering a delightful fusion of Southern, Caribbean, and Latin American flavors. The restaurant is known for its flavorful dishes like Bahamian Chicken Curry, Calypso Nachos, and the highly praised Georgia Peach Pound Cake. With options like coconut curry and sesame-crusted catfish, the menu emphasizes a balance of textures and bold tastes. The outdoor seating, under old oak trees, adds charm to the dining experience, while the restaurant's relaxed, dog-friendly patio appeals to many. Seating is limited and includes just one restroom, so it may get busy, particularly after being featured on the popular show *Diners, Drive-Ins, and Dives.*

Nearby Attractions:

- **Mary Ross Waterfront Park:** A scenic spot to explore near downtown Brunswick.

- **Historic Ritz Theatre:** Offering entertainment and performances within close proximity.

Important Information for Visitors:
Plan to arrive early for seating, particularly during peak times, due to limited capacity.

Vic's On the River

Location: 26 E Bay St, Floor 2, Rousakis Riverfront Plaza, Savannah, GA 31401, United States
Plus Code: 3WJ5+FV Savannah, Georgia, USA
Contact: +1 912-721-1000
Website: vicsontheriver.com

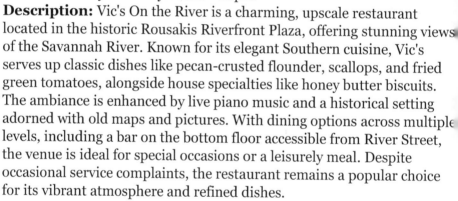

Opening Hours:
- Saturday to Friday: 11am – 10pm

Description: Vic's On the River is a charming, upscale restaurant located in the historic Rousakis Riverfront Plaza, offering stunning views of the Savannah River. Known for its elegant Southern cuisine, Vic's serves up classic dishes like pecan-crusted flounder, scallops, and fried green tomatoes, alongside house specialties like honey butter biscuits. The ambiance is enhanced by live piano music and a historical setting adorned with old maps and pictures. With dining options across multiple levels, including a bar on the bottom floor accessible from River Street, the venue is ideal for special occasions or a leisurely meal. Despite occasional service complaints, the restaurant remains a popular choice for its vibrant atmosphere and refined dishes.

Nearby Attractions:

- **Savannah Riverfront:** A scenic spot with beautiful views and shopping along River Street.

- **Johnson Square:** A historical landmark just a short walk away.

Important Information for Visitors:
Reservations are recommended due to the restaurant's popularity, particularly for special occasions. Ensure to request a seating preference

if ambiance and location within the restaurant are important to your dining experience.

Props Steak and Seafood Restaurant

Location:
1289 S Houston Lake Rd, Warner Robins, GA 31088, United States
Plus Code: H84P+QR Warner Robins, Georgia, USA
Contact: +1 478-224-7767
Website: propswr.com
Opening Hours:

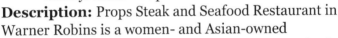

- Saturday: 11am – 10pm
- Sunday to Thursday: 11am – 9pm
- Friday: 11am – 10pm

Description: Props Steak and Seafood Restaurant in Warner Robins is a women- and Asian-owned establishment celebrated for its premium steaks and diverse seafood options. Known for its welcoming service and vibrant atmosphere, it offers a wide-ranging menu that includes dishes like ribeye steaks, stuffed chicken, herb-crusted salmon, and seafood staples such as shrimp and scallops. Diners appreciate the generous portions and variety, though some find the pricing on the higher end, particularly for steaks. Props also features a popular dessert selection, including donut bread pudding. Ideal for family dinners or special occasions, large parties should anticipate a gratuity rate and potentially longer wait times during peak hours.

Nearby Attractions:

- **Museum of Aviation:** One of Georgia's top tourist attractions, located a short drive away.

- **Rigby's Entertainment Complex:** Offers bowling, arcade games, and more for family fun.

Important Information for Visitors:
Props adds a 20% gratuity for parties of five or more. It is recommended to visit outside peak times if you prefer faster seating and service. There is ample free parking available on site.

Nino's Italian Restaurant

Location:
1931 Cheshire Bridge Rd NE, Atlanta,
GA 30324, United States
Plus Code: RJ6R+25 Atlanta,
Georgia, USA
Contact: +1 404-874-6505
Website:
ninosatlanta.com

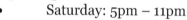

Opening Hours:

- Saturday: 5pm – 11pm
- Sunday: 11:30am – 3pm, 5pm – 10pm
- Monday: Closed (Labor Day)
- Tuesday to Thursday: 11:30am – 2pm, 5pm – 10pm
- Friday: 5pm – 11pm

Description: Nino's Italian Restaurant is a long-standing Atlanta institution that exudes the charm of a classic Italian dining experience. Established on Cheshire Bridge Road, Nino's features traditional Italian fare with a modern touch. The menu highlights include pasta dishes such as calamarata with rapini and sausage, pasta al limone reminiscent of Italy's Amalfi Coast, and seafood specialties like baked clams. Guests praise the inviting atmosphere, welcoming service from the hostess Alessandra and chef Micah, and the bar's bright, refreshed look. While some have noted slow service during busy times or large parties, the quality of food, including freshly prepared sauces and desserts, remains a consistent draw for diners.

Nearby Attractions:

- **Atlanta Botanical Garden:** A beautiful urban oasis featuring a range of plant collections and sculptures, located within a short drive.

- **Piedmont Park:** A large park with walking trails, sports facilities, and seasonal events, ideal for a pre- or post-dinner stroll.

Important Information for Visitors:
Expect slow service during peak hours, particularly when large parties are present. Reservations are recommended for a smooth dining experience. Nino's identifies as both Black-owned and LGBTQ+ friendly, contributing to its welcoming environment.

C&S Seafood & Oyster Bar

Location:
6125 Roswell Rd, Suite 700,
Sandy Springs, GA 30328,
United States
Located in: The Morgan Sandy
Springs
Plus Code: WJCC+RF Sandy
Springs, Georgia, USA
Contact: +1 470-427-3826

Website: candsoysterbar.com

Opening Hours:
*   Saturday: 11am – 11pm
*   Sunday: 11am – 10pm
*   Monday to Thursday: 4pm – 10pm
*   Friday: 11am – 11pm

Description: C&S Seafood & Oyster Bar in Sandy Springs offers an upscale dining experience with a focus on high-quality seafood. Known for its exceptional service, led by attentive staff like Jeremiah and Bridget, and a welcoming atmosphere, the restaurant excels in dishes like chargrilled oysters, red snapper, grouper, and grilled jumbo shrimp with lemon herb sauce. Popular for date nights, family dinners, and special occasions, C&S features a modern ambiance that complements its extensive seafood menu. However, diners have noted occasional inconsistencies with food temperature and plating. Valet parking is available for $3, making it a convenient option for guests.

Nearby Attractions:

*   **Chattahoochee River National Recreation Area:** A natural getaway offering hiking trails and river views, ideal for a relaxing visit before or after dining.

Important Information for Visitors:
Reservations are recommended, especially during peak hours. Valet parking is available for $3, and there is free street parking and a lot. Some guests have mentioned that the restaurant's seating and service can vary, so patience during busy times is advised.

Bones Restaurant

Location: 3130 Piedmont Rd NE, Atlanta, GA 30305, United States
Plus Code:
QM75+44 Atlanta, Georgia, USA
Contact: +1 404-237-2663
Website: bonesrestaurant.com
Opening Hours:

- Monday to Thursday: 5:30pm – 10pm
- Friday and Saturday: 5:30pm – 11pm
- Sunday: Closed

Description: Bones Restaurant, one of Atlanta's most celebrated steakhouses, offers a classic fine dining experience that exudes sophistication and tradition. Known for its exceptional service and high-quality steaks, Bones has been an Atlanta institution for decades. Whether celebrating a special occasion or indulging in a fine dining experience, guests are treated to a carefully curated menu featuring premium steaks, seafood, and expertly prepared sides such as hash brown potatoes and asparagus. The service is top-tier, with attentive staff providing a seamless dining experience. Signature dishes include the wagyu carpaccio, lobster bisque, and the New York strip steak.

While highly praised for its ambiance and service, some guests note that the high prices ($140+ per person) may not always justify the food quality, especially the desserts, which are less favored. The restaurant is an iconic must-try for steak lovers, though it may be a one-time bucket-list experience for some.

Nearby Attractions:

- **Atlanta History Center:** A historical museum with exhibitions covering the Civil War, Southern culture, and regional history.

Important Information for Visitors:
Bones is a high-end dining venue with a focus on traditional steakhouse fare. Due to its popularity, reservations are highly recommended, especially for special occasions. The small, cozy setting adds to its charm, but be prepared for a more intimate dining environment.

SOHO Atlanta Restaurant

Location:
4300 Paces Ferry Rd SE #107, Atlanta, GA 30339, United States
Located in Vinings Jubilee
Plus Code:
VG8M+88 Atlanta, Georgia, USA
Contact: +1 770-801-0069
Website:
sohoatlanta.com
Opening Hours:
- Saturday: 5pm – 10pm
- Sunday: 5pm – 9pm
- Monday (Labor Day): 5pm – 9pm
- Tuesday to Thursday: 5pm – 9pm
- Friday: 5pm – 10pm

Description: SOHO Atlanta Restaurant, nestled in Vinings Jubilee, offers a warm and inviting dining experience with a focus on globally inspired cuisine. The restaurant is known for its exceptional service, ensuring that guests enjoy a memorable meal from start to finish. The menu boasts a variety of standout dishes, including The General's Calamari, Burgundy Braised Short Rib, Ahi Tuna, and Crab Crusted Salmon, which have garnered praise for their flavors and presentation. For dessert, the chocolate bread pudding is a highly recommended must-try.

With a blend of comforting dishes such as the Blue Plate Chicken and house-made pasta, SOHO caters to diverse palates, making it a great spot for both casual dining and special occasions. The ambiance complements the well-crafted menu, making it a popular destination in the Vinings area.

Nearby Attractions:

- **Cumberland Mall:** A popular shopping destination with a range of retail stores and dining options.

- **Silver Comet Trail:** A scenic walking and biking trail located nearby, perfect for outdoor enthusiasts.

SOUVENIRS & GIFTS

City Souvenirs & Gifts LLC

Location: 5738 Buford Hwy NE, Doraville, GA 30340, United States

Plus Code: WP5J+C6 Doraville, Georgia, USA

Contact: +1 770-986-0981

Opening Hours:

- Saturday: 11 am – 3 pm
- Sunday: 10 am – 5 pm
- Monday (Labor Day): 10 am – 5:30 pm (Hours might differ)
- Tuesday to Friday: 10 am – 5:30 pm

Description: City Souvenirs & Gifts LLC is located in the Doraville Plaza Shopping Center and offers a variety of souvenirs including keychains, magnets, and photo frames. This shop is known for its diverse selection and reasonable prices. They provide discounts for bulk purchases and occasionally offer complimentary gifts. The shop's welcoming environment and helpful staff make it a convenient choice for picking up gifts for loved ones.

Georgia Gifts & More

Location: 5001 Lavista Rd Ste A, Tucker, GA 30084, United States
Plus Code: VQ3M+RF Tucker, Georgia, USA
Contact: +1 404-241-1375
Website: www.georgiagiftsandmore.com
Opening Hours: 11 am – 6 pm

Description: Georgia Gifts & More is a small store offering a wide range of local Georgia souvenirs, including jams, snacks, prints, candles, gift baskets, books, and t-shirts. Located in Tucker, this shop is known for its friendly staff and diverse selection of items, from handcrafted goods to common souvenirs. It is a popular choice for finding authentic Georgia gifts as well as more standard items like magnets and pens. The store provides a welcoming environment for visitors looking for unique Georgia memorabilia.

Sand Dollars Gift Shop

Location: 225 Baker St NW, Atlanta, GA 30313, United States
Plus Code: QJ74+72 Atlanta, Georgia, USA
Description: Sand Dollars Gift Shop, located on the first floor of the Georgia Aquarium, offers a variety of souvenirs related to the aquarium experience. Visitors can choose from a selection of toys, shirts, jewelry, and other items. The shop provides fair pricing, reflecting its role in supporting the aquarium's operations. It is a convenient spot for picking up memorabilia from a visit to the aquarium.

Atlanta Souvenirs LLC

Location: 221 Baker St NW, Atlanta, GA 30313, United States
Plus Code: QJ64+W7 Atlanta, Georgia, USA
Contact: +1 404-999-1014
Opening Hours: 12 pm – 6 pm Tuesday: Closed
Description: Atlanta Souvenirs LLC is located on the first floor of Centennial Olympic Park and offers a range of souvenirs with reasonable pricing. The shop features a variety of items that make ideal keepsakes from a visit to the park. Known for its good service and polite staff, the store provides a convenient option for finding souvenirs in a popular tourist area.

State Botanical Garden of Georgia Gift Shop

Location: Visitor Center & Conservatory, 2450 S Milledge Ave, Athens, GA 30605, United States
Plus Code: WJ28+FH Athens, Georgia, USA
Contact: +1 706-542-6159
Website: botgarden.uga.edu
Opening Hours:
- Saturday: 10 am – 4 pm
- Sunday: 12 pm – 4 pm
- Monday to Friday: 10 am – 4 pm

Description: The State Botanical Garden of Georgia Gift Shop is located within the Visitor Center and Conservatory of the garden. The shop offers a variety of nature-themed gifts and souvenirs, ideal for visitors exploring the beautiful gardens. Items include garden-related gifts, local crafts, and educational materials. The shop supports the garden's mission and provides a pleasant shopping experience for guests.

Georgia Aquarium Gift Shop

Location: 225 Baker St NW, Atlanta, GA 30313, United States
Plus Code: QJ73+9X Atlanta, Georgia, USA
Website: www.georgiaaquarium.org

Description: The Georgia Aquarium Gift Shop, located on the first floor of the Georgia Aquarium, offers a variety of marine-themed souvenirs and gifts. Visitors can find an array of items including plush toys, books, and other memorabilia featuring sea creatures. The shop is colorful and expansive, catering to marine enthusiasts and those looking for unique keepsakes from their aquarium visit. It provides a fun and engaging shopping experience for guests exploring the aquarium.

Georgia Artisan Center

Location: 99 N Armed Forces Blvd, Warner Robins, GA 31093, United States
Plus Code: J9CX+2X Warner Robins, Georgia, USA
Contact: +1 770-376-7324
Website: visitwarnerrobins.org

Opening Hours:
- Saturday: Closed
- Sunday: Closed
- Monday to Friday: 8 am – 5 pm

Description: The Georgia Artisan Center, located on N Armed Forces Blvd, offers a selection of handmade and locally crafted items. The center is known for its friendly and helpful staff, who provide visitors with information about local attractions and events. It features a variety of Georgia-made goods, including unique and artisanal products. Prices may be higher due to the handmade nature of the items. The center also hosts raffles and provides brochures on local attractions.

Grace Quinn Gifts & More

Location: 154 S Houston Lake Rd #500, Warner Robins, GA 31088, United States
Plus Code: J87C+G5 Warner Robins, Georgia, USA
Contact: +1 478-333-1731
Website: m.facebook.com
Opening Hours:

- Saturday: 9 am – 3 pm
- Sunday: Closed
- Monday to Friday: 10 am – 3 pm

Description: Grace Quinn Gifts & More is located on S Houston Lake Rd and offers a range of gifts and custom products. Known for its personalized service and quality craftsmanship, the shop features custom shirts, accessories, and a variety of other items. The owner is recognized for her attentive and quick service, ensuring a pleasant shopping experience. The store is ideal for those looking for unique and well-made gifts, including personalized options.

Crazy Daisy Gift Shop

Location: 1499 US-280, Pembroke, GA 31321, United States
Plus Code: 4CM2+PX Pembroke, Georgia, USA
Contact: +1 912-653-4438
Opening Hours:

- Saturday: Closed
- Sunday: Closed
- Monday to Friday: 9 am – 5 pm

Description: Crazy Daisy Gift Shop is located on US-280 in Pembroke and offers a variety of stylish

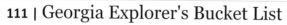

and unique gifts. The shop features a range of items including custom embroidery and vinyl monograms. Known for its friendly service and reasonable prices, it provides a welcoming atmosphere for visitors seeking distinctive gifts and personalized products.

Whistle Stop Cafe Gift Shop

Location: 446 McCrackin St, Juliette, GA 31046, United States
Plus Code: 4642+H9 Juliette, Georgia, USA
Contact: +1 478-992-8886
Website: thewhistlestopcafe.com
Opening Hours:
- Saturday: 11 am – 4 pm
- Sunday: 11 am – 4 pm
- Tuesday: Closed
- Wednesday: Closed
- Thursday to Friday: 11 am – 4 pm

Description: The Whistle Stop Cafe Gift Shop, located in Juliette, offers a variety of gifts and souvenirs. Situated next to the cafe, which is known for its country-style food, the gift shop features items related to the cafe's theme and local area. It provides a unique shopping experience with a range of memorabilia and locally inspired gifts, reflecting the charm of the surrounding town.

ITINERARY

3-Day Itinerary for Georgia

Day 1: Atlanta's Highlights and Historical Gems

Morning:

- **Centennial Olympic Park**
  Start your day at **Centennial Olympic Park**, a vibrant downtown park built for the 1996 Summer Olympics. Stroll through the park, enjoy the **Fountain of Rings**, and take in views of the city skyline.
- **Georgia Aquarium**
  Just a short walk from the park, visit the **Georgia Aquarium**, one of the largest aquariums in the world. It houses more than 100,000 animals, including whale sharks, beluga whales, and manta rays.

Afternoon:

- **Delta Flight Museum**
  Head to the **Delta Flight Museum** for an immersive experience in aviation history. Located near Hartsfield-Jackson Airport, this museum showcases the rich history of Delta Airlines, with interactive exhibits and historic planes.
- **Tank Town USA**
  In the afternoon, venture to **Tank Town USA** for a fun, adrenaline-filled experience. You can drive real military tanks or enjoy an off-road adventure, making it an exciting attraction for visitors seeking something unique.

Evening:

- **Fun Spot America Theme Parks — Atlanta**
  End your day at **Fun Spot America**, a family-friendly
  amusement park in Atlanta. Ride roller coasters, try go-
  karting, or play classic arcade games to round out an
  exciting first day.

Day 2: Exploring Savannah's Charm and Coastal Beauty

Morning:

- **Savannah Historic District**
  Begin your day by exploring the **Savannah Historic
  District**, one of the largest National Historic Landmark
  districts in the United States. Stroll down cobblestone
  streets, admire the antebellum architecture, and visit
  beautiful public squares like **Reynolds Square,
  Oglethorpe Square**, and **Madison Square**.
- **River Street Savannah Georgia**
  After exploring the historic district, head to **River Street**,
  a bustling waterfront lined with shops, restaurants, and
  art galleries. Enjoy a leisurely walk and take in views of
  the Savannah River.

Afternoon:

- **Skidaway Island State Park**
  Drive to **Skidaway Island State Park**, a peaceful coastal
  park that offers scenic hiking trails through maritime
  forests and salt marshes. The park is perfect for nature
  lovers looking to escape the hustle and bustle of the city.
- **Fort McAllister State Park**
  Visit **Fort McAllister State Park**, home to one of the best-
  preserved Civil War-era earthwork forts. Learn about

Georgia's Civil War history, walk through the museum, and enjoy the surrounding natural beauty.

Evening:

- **Driftwood Beach**
  Wrap up the day with a sunset visit to **Driftwood Beach**, one of the most photographed spots on Jekyll Island. The unique, weathered trees make this beach a mesmerizing location for photos and peaceful reflection.

Day 3: Nature, History, and Coastal Attractions

Morning:

- **Ocmulgee Mounds National Historical Park**
  Start your day by heading to **Ocmulgee Mounds National Historical Park** in Macon, which showcases thousands of years of Native American history. Explore the mounds, the Earth Lodge, and enjoy walking trails around this historically significant site.
- **Providence Canyon State Park**
  Next, drive to **Providence Canyon State Park**, also known as Georgia's "Little Grand Canyon." The colorful canyons make for fantastic photo opportunities, and you can enjoy several hiking trails that take you through the canyon's unique landscape.

Afternoon:

- **F.D. Roosevelt State Park**
  Visit **F.D. Roosevelt State Park**, Georgia's largest state park, where you can hike to scenic overlooks, enjoy a picnic, or take in the views of Dowdell's Knob, one of President Roosevelt's favorite spots.
- **Fort Frederica National Monument**
  Head to the coast and explore **Fort Frederica National**

Monument on St. Simons Island. This historic site was once a British fort and settlement. Walk through the ruins, learn about the colonial era, and take in the beauty of the surrounding marshlands.

Evening:

- **Golden Isles Convention & Visitors Bureau**
  Finish your 3-day adventure by visiting the **Golden Isles Convention & Visitors Bureau** to gather more information on the Golden Isles and nearby attractions. It's a perfect way to end your trip with ideas for future explorations of Georgia's coastal wonders.

Optional Additions for Extra Time:

- **Little Cumberland Island Lighthouse**
  If you're near the coast, you may want to visit the **Little Cumberland Island Lighthouse**, a historic lighthouse that offers great views and rich maritime history.
- **Southern Forest World**
  For those interested in nature and forestry, **Southern Forest World** is a unique museum dedicated to the history of Georgia's forests.

7-Day Itinerary for Georgia

Day 1: Explore Atlanta's Major Attractions

Morning:

- **Centennial Olympic Park**
  Kick off your trip at **Centennial Olympic Park**, the heart

of downtown Atlanta. Enjoy a morning walk through the park, taking in the **Fountain of Rings** and reflecting on Atlanta's Olympic history.

- **Georgia Aquarium**
Right next door is the **Georgia Aquarium**, where you'll be amazed by the sheer size and variety of marine life, including whale sharks, dolphins, and sea otters.

Afternoon:

- **Delta Flight Museum**
Explore the history of aviation at the **Delta Flight Museum**. This museum offers a unique look at Delta Airlines' history, complete with interactive exhibits and historic aircraft.

Evening:

- **Fun Spot America Theme Parks — Atlanta**
Finish your day at **Fun Spot America**, an amusement park that's perfect for families. Try the go-karts, roller coasters, and arcade games.

Day 2: Atlanta's Historic Sites & Family Fun

Morning:

- **Stone Mountain Park**
Start the day at **Stone Mountain Park**, one of Georgia's most famous landmarks. Ride the Summit Skyride to the top for panoramic views, hike the mountain, or explore the Confederate Memorial Carving.

Afternoon:

- **Jimmy Carter National Historical Park**
Head to **Jimmy Carter National Historical Park** to learn about the 39th U.S. president. The museum and

Carter's boyhood home offer fascinating insights into his life and presidency.

Evening:

- **Barbie Beach**
  Wrap up the day with a quirky stop at **Barbie Beach**. This unusual roadside attraction features dozens of Barbie dolls in various displays, offering a fun and lighthearted experience.

Day 3: Savannah's Historic Charm

Morning:

- **Savannah Historic District**
  Spend the morning exploring the **Savannah Historic District**, with its charming squares, historic homes, and stunning architecture. Don't miss **Oglethorpe Square**, **Reynolds Square**, and **Madison Square**.
- **River Street Savannah Georgia**
  Afterward, head to **River Street** for a leisurely stroll along the Savannah River. Enjoy shopping, dining, and watching the ships go by.

Afternoon:

- **Skidaway Island State Park**
  Just outside of Savannah, **Skidaway Island State Park** offers serene hiking trails through marshlands and maritime forests. It's a great spot to take in the coastal beauty of Georgia.

Evening:

- **Savannah Children's Museum**
  If you're traveling with kids, spend the evening at the

Savannah Children's Museum. This outdoor museum offers hands-on exhibits and interactive fun.

Day 4: Coastal Georgia & Historical Sites

Morning:

- **Fort Frederica National Monument**
  Drive to St. Simons Island to visit **Fort Frederica National Monument**. This historic site includes the ruins of a British fort and settlement from the colonial era.
- **Golden Isles Convention & Visitors Bureau**
  Stop by the **Golden Isles Convention & Visitors Bureau** to get information about exploring Georgia's coastal islands, like Jekyll and St. Simons.

Afternoon:

- **Driftwood Beach**
  Head to **Driftwood Beach** on Jekyll Island, one of Georgia's most picturesque spots. Walk along the beach and marvel at the weathered trees that give it a surreal, otherworldly feel.

Evening:

- **Old Fort Jackson**
  Back in Savannah, visit **Old Fort Jackson**, a well-preserved fort from the War of 1812. Witness live cannon firings and enjoy the scenic views of the Savannah River.

Day 5: Explore Georgia's Nature & State Parks

Morning:

- **Providence Canyon State Park**
  Venture to **Providence Canyon State Park**, known as Georgia's "Little Grand Canyon." The striking orange and red canyon walls make for stunning photography, and there are multiple hiking trails to explore.

Afternoon:

- **F.D. Roosevelt State Park**
  Visit **F.D. Roosevelt State Park**, Georgia's largest state park. Enjoy scenic hikes and stunning overlooks, including Dowdell's Knob, a favorite spot of President Roosevelt.

Evening:

- **Fort McAllister State Park**
  Return to the coast to visit **Fort McAllister State Park**, a Civil War-era fort surrounded by beautiful marshes. Explore the museum and walk the well-preserved grounds.

Day 6: Unique Experiences and Coastal Wonders

Morning:

- **Ocmulgee Mounds National Historical Park**
  Head to Macon to explore **Ocmulgee Mounds National Historical Park**, where you can learn about 17,000 years of Native American history. Walk the trails and visit the ancient mounds.

Afternoon:

- **Little Cumberland Island Lighthouse**
  Drive to **Little Cumberland Island** and visit the **Little Cumberland Island Lighthouse**, one of the oldest lighthouses in the state. The remote island and the lighthouse make for a peaceful and scenic experience.

Evening:

- **Phantom Manor**
  For a spooky twist, check out **Phantom Manor**, a haunted attraction known for its eerie atmosphere and thrilling experiences.

Day 7: History and Offbeat Attractions

Morning:

- **Cannonball House**
  Start your final day with a visit to **Cannonball House** in Macon, which survived a cannonball strike during the Civil War. The house offers tours and historical insights into Georgia's Civil War history.
- **Jarrell Plantation State Historic Site**
  Drive to **Jarrell Plantation State Historic Site**, a well-preserved 19th-century cotton plantation. Explore the historic buildings and learn about plantation life in Georgia.

Afternoon:

- **Southern Forest World**
  Visit **Southern Forest World** in Waycross, a museum dedicated to Georgia's timber industry and forestry history. It's a unique and educational stop for those interested in nature and conservation.

Evening:

- **Tank Town USA**
  End your trip with some adventure at **Tank Town USA**, where you can drive a real tank or crush cars. It's an exhilarating experience to cap off your Georgia journey!

"DID YOU KNOW?" FACTS ABOUT GEORGIA

1. Did You Know? Georgia is known as the "Peach State," but it's actually the country's top producer of peanuts, pecans, and Vidalia onions.

2. Did You Know? The **Georgia Aquarium** in Atlanta is one of the largest aquariums in the world, housing more than 100,000 aquatic animals, including whale sharks.

3. Did You Know? **Savannah**, Georgia's oldest city, is home to one of the largest National Historic Landmark Districts in the United States, with cobblestone streets and beautiful public squares.

4. Did You Know? Georgia is the birthplace of **Martin Luther King Jr.**, and you can visit his childhood home and the **Martin Luther King Jr. National Historical Park** in Atlanta.

5. Did You Know? The world-famous soft drink **Coca-Cola** was invented in Atlanta by pharmacist John Stith Pemberton in 1886. You can explore its history at the **World of Coca-Cola** museum.

6. Did You Know? Georgia's **Stone Mountain** has the largest exposed granite dome in North America, and its Confederate Memorial Carving is one of the largest bas-relief sculptures in the world.

7. Did You Know? Georgia's **Little Grand Canyon**, also known as **Providence Canyon State Park**, was actually formed by poor farming practices in the 1800s, not natural erosion.

8. Did You Know? The **Big Oak** in Thomasville, Georgia, is more than 330 years old and has a limb span of 162 feet, making it one of the largest Southern live oaks in the country.

9. Did You Know? Georgia is home to **Jekyll Island**, once a private retreat for some of America's wealthiest families, including the Rockefellers, Morgans, and Vanderbilts.

10. Did You Know? **Jimmy Carter**, the 39th president of the United States, hails from Plains, Georgia, and the town features

the **Jimmy Carter National Historical Park**, dedicated to his life and legacy.

11. Did You Know? **Fort Frederica National Monument** on St. Simons Island preserves the remnants of an early British colonial settlement and fort from the 18th century.

12. Did You Know? The town of **Helen**, Georgia, is a re-creation of a Bavarian Alpine village, complete with cobblestone streets and German-inspired architecture, drawing thousands of tourists annually.

13. Did You Know? **Driftwood Beach** on Jekyll Island is renowned for its picturesque driftwood trees, making it a popular spot for photographers and nature lovers.

14. Did You Know? Georgia's **Ocmulgee Mounds National Historical Park** contains evidence of 17,000 years of continuous human habitation, including ancient Native American mounds.

15. Did You Know? **F.D. Roosevelt State Park** is Georgia's largest state park, named after the 32nd president, who frequented the nearby **Warm Springs** for therapy during his battle with polio.

16. Did You Know? The **Golden Isles** of Georgia (St. Simons, Sea Island, Jekyll, and Little St. Simons) are known for their pristine beaches, wildlife, and Gilded Age history.

17. Did You Know? The **Atlanta Cyclorama & Civil War Museum** houses one of the world's largest oil paintings, depicting the 1864 Battle of Atlanta during the Civil War.

18. Did You Know? **Phinizy Swamp Nature Park** in Augusta is a vast wetland park home to unique bird species, amphibians, and plant life, offering scenic nature trails and environmental education programs.

19. Did You Know? Georgia's **Providence Canyon** boasts stunning red, orange, and pink soil layers that create breathtaking vistas, often referred to as Georgia's "Little Grand Canyon."

20. Did You Know? Georgia is home to **Tank Town USA**, where you can drive real military tanks and even crush cars, offering a truly unique adventure for thrill-seekers!

TRAVEL

DATE:

DURATION:

DESTINATION:

PLACES TO SEE:

1 _____
2 _____
3 _____
4 _____
5 _____
6 _____
7 _____

LOCAL FOOD TO TRY:

1 _____
2 _____
3 _____
4 _____
5 _____
6 _____
7 _____

NOTES

EXPENSES IN TOTAL:

JOURNAL

TRAVEL

DATE:

DURATION:

DESTINATION:

PLACES TO SEE:	LOCAL FOOD TO TRY:
1 _____	1 _____
2 _____	2 _____
3 _____	3 _____
4 _____	4 _____
5 _____	5 _____
6 _____	6 _____
7 _____	7 _____

NOTES

EXPENSES IN TOTAL:

JOURNAL

TRAVEL

DATE:

DURATION:

DESTINATION:

PLACES TO SEE:

1 _____
2 _____
3 _____
4 _____
5 _____
6 _____
7 _____

LOCAL FOOD TO TRY:

1 _____
2 _____
3 _____
4 _____
5 _____
6 _____
7 _____

NOTES

EXPENSES IN TOTAL:

JOURNAL

Made in United States
Orlando, FL
15 December 2024